Law
and
Psychology
in
Conflict

Second Edition

Law and Psychology in Conflict

Second Edition

By JAMES MARSHALL

THE BOBBS-MERRILL COMPANY, INC.

Publishers

INDIANAPOLIS • NEW YORK • CHARLOTTESVILLE, VIRGINIA

To my grandchildren and to Liza and Eva, with love and hope.

FOREWORD TO SECOND EDITION

In the intervening years since the first edition of this book in 1966, there has been considerably increased research in the area of law and psychology. A number of important court decisions have emphasized discrepancies between law and psychology. As the first edition of this book has been quoted, cited, mentioned in footnotes and sometimes reproduced in part by law schools (without the author's or publisher's permission), it seems appropriate to bring out a more up-to-date edition.

This book does not purport to cover all relevant cases, legal literature or psychological research concerning psychology and law. It does not deal with a number of conflict areas such as testimony by expert witnesses and intention. To give consideration to all of this material might result in a more scholarly volume but probably at the cost of interest and stimulation. It is hoped that some of the vital conflicts between the two disciplines will be here opened up to encourage further research by lawyers and psychologists, or better by teams of both.

I apologize for the footnotes. Lawyers are so dependent on authority that they do not trust a statement not anchored to what someone else has written. I have heard of legal publications that will not accept a manuscript lean of footnotes. Social scientists tend to be satisfied with references to the bibliography. Only an explanatory or witty footnote should be tolerated.

"Of making many books there is no end", we are told; and in a world of increasing knowledge and its application there should be no end — and cannot be in a society founded on freedom of thought and communication. May there be no end to books and other publications based on empirical studies of conflicts between law and social-science findings.

J.M.

vii

FOREWORD TO FIRST EDITION

Man's ability to think depends almost wholly on his ability to observe and recall what he has observed. Logic is a futile and arid exercise without data. But we have no data save by the evidence of our senses. So the reliability of evidence provided by human senses is fundamental to rational thought.

It is no new discovery that our senses often mislead us and that the data provided by observation and recall are often in error. Since antiquity men have been conscious of deficiencies in their data, although only the most thoughtful were aware of the extent of these deficiencies. In the Seventh Book of Plato's *Republic*, Socrates likens human beings to prisoners living in an underground den who have been chained since childhood so they cannot move or turn their heads and who can see only the wall of the cave. The cave has a mouth open toward the light and a fire is blazing at a distance. Between the fire and the prisoners there is a path along which men pass, carrying all sorts of vessels and statues and figures made of various materials. The prisoners see only the shadows which the fire throws on the opposite wall of the cave. To them the truth is literally nothing but the shadows of images. Then, Socrates continues in the dialogue, see what would follow if the prisoners were released and disabused of their error. When first liberated and compelled to turn around and look toward the light one would suffer sharp pains; the glare would distress him; and he would be unable to see the realities of which in his former state he had seen the shadows. If someone would say to him that what he saw before was an illusion but that now when his eye is turned toward more real existence he has a clearer vision, he will fancy that the shadows which he formerly saw are truer than the objects which are now shown to him. And if he is compelled to look straight at the light, he will have a pain in his eyes which will make him turn away to take refuge in the objects of vision which he can see, and which he will conceive to be in reality clearer than the things which are now being shown to him.

Although the author of this book does not invoke the Platonic metaphor, the message of this book is that our courts are in the position of the prisoners of the cave. As I have pointed out elsewhere,[1] law suits are never decided on the facts since only evidence is available to the courts and this is simply a secondary indication of the facts.

In this book, Mr. Marshall shows us how the courts, both judges and juries, are like Plato's prisoners of the cave in that they watch the shadows on the wall and discuss with one another what the "reality" of the shadow is. The main burden of this book is to show that there is now a substantial body of scientific information to establish the lack of correspondence between the shadows on the wall (or the testimony in court) and the actual figures passing before the opening of the cave (that is, the events with which the law suit is concerned). The data of experimental psychology now establish quite securely that no two individuals observe any complex occurrence in quite the same manner; that the ability of different individuals to retain and recall observations differs; that the elements which are retained and recalled are influenced by past experience and attitudes; and that the ability of various individuals to express what they have observed, retained and recalled varies greatly. There is no wholly reliable witness since the observation of all witnesses is faulty in some degree and some situations.

In the intellectual history of mankind, the two principal methods developed for securing and testing data have been scientific research and the adversary trial. By and large these have been used in different situations and have different purposes. For reasons that are not very readily apparent, the fact-finding processes of science and of law have had relatively little effect upon one another. The message that Mr. Marshall brings in this book is that this condition cannot continue. He gathers here the results of most of the scientific work that has been done in the field of evidentiary reliability and includes a report of an interesting original experiment of his own in this area. The conclusion which he reaches is that the scientific data now known make "acute the need for a complete reconsideration of the rules of evidence to conform them overall instead of piecemeal to what we know of the human condition." Few scholars of the law of evidence will quarrel with this conclusion. But more than the scholars should be concerned. Lawyers, legislators and informed citizens should be

---

[1] Loevinger, *Facts, Evidence and Legal Proof,* 9 W. Res. L. Rev. 154 (1958); Henson, Landmarks of Law 422 (1960).

aware of the problems inherent in the investigation of facts by human testimony. This volume not only makes it possible for everyone to gain this insight but also makes it an interesting, and even exciting, intellectual experience. No attempt is made here to present any authoritative or official answers, for none are yet available to most of the problems examined. What the author does do is to present the questions and problems that must be considered if law is to continue to perform its central function in our society.

There will, no doubt, be lawyers and judges who will react to material in this book as Plato's prisoners of the cave reacted to the sunlight and the sight of the world of solid objects which they had previously seen only by shadow. Some will insist that we must rely on testimony and that, since we do not know the precise limits of its accuracy, we should ignore its defects and limitations. As Plato observed so long ago, to those accustomed to darkness the light is painful, to those accustomed to shadows solid objects are unreal. But light has the power to dispel darkness and shadows are no match for solid objects. There is no choice in this matter. We may ignore reality but we cannot escape it. This book is an effort to help us face the ubiquitous problem of making evidence correspond with facts. This is a challenge to all who are concerned with the processes of law. It is also the first task of any man who would be rational in his approach to the world.

Lee Loevinger

ACKNOWLEDGEMENTS

The Author gratefully acknowledges the assistance of the following:

The late Professor Arthur R. Cohen, who was helpful in discussing the plan of this book; Professors Hadley Cantril and Henry H. Foster, Jr., Gerhardt Mueller, Isidor Chein and Alfred Cohn for their advice; and Mrs. Sarah Katz for the difficult job of typing and arranging the book and disentangling the Author's notes.

In connection with research in Chapter III, the Author is indebted to Dr. Helge Mansson, who conducted the experiments reported jointly with the Author, and John VanEsen, for his careful and laborious technical help; Miss Helen Hall and Mr. Felipe Ortez, for help in the experiment at the Henry Street Settlement, Chief Deputy Inspector George P. McManus and Captains Vincent T. Agoglis and Joseph A. Preiss, in connection with the experiment at the New York Police Academy; to Mrs. Keitha Parnes, for rating answers to the questionnaires; and the National Broadcasting Company and Lawrence K. Grossman, for the film used.

Thanks also go to Kent H. Marquis and Stuart Oskamp for their collaboration (and good fellowship) in the experiment reported in Chapter IV, and to The Harvard Law Review Association for permission to quote material first appearing in THE HARVARD LAW REVIEW, (copyrighted 1971).

CONTENTS

ILLUSTRATIONS

INTRODUCTION

Explaining his difficulties with the evidence on which he based his conclusions, Thucydides talked of "the want of coincidence between accounts of the same occurrences by different eyewitnesses, arising sometimes from imperfect memory, sometimes from undue partiality for one side or the other." Of the speeches which he reported, some of which he had himself heard, some of which he had heard from others, he wrote that "It was in all cases difficult to carry them word for word in one's memory, so my habit has been to make the speakers say what was in my opinion demanded of them by the various occasions, of course adhering as closely as possible to the general sense of what they really said." [1]

Thucydides' difficulty in discerning the realities of events from eyewitnesses and those who had heard relevant statements plagues the law of evidence today. His experiences with the problem of arriving at reality from his own and others' memories have been validated by the findings of modern psychology. The very perceptions on which recollection is founded tend to be inaccurate, for they reflect not so much the objective qualities of what has been seen and heard as the expectations or preconceptions that the observer brings to the event and his "transactions" or interactions with others who may have been involved.

For the law, the basic problem of truth does not arise so much from the villainy of perjurers and suborners of perjury as from the unreliability of personal observation. As Shaw said in his "Introduction" to *Saint Joan,* "It is what men do at their best, with good intentions, and what normal men and women find that they must and will do in spite of their intentions, that really concern us." [2]

---

[1] THUCYDIDES, COMPLETE WRITINGS 14 (Modern Library ed. Crawley transl. 1951).

[2] SHAW, SAINT JOAN 51 (Modern Library ed. 1956).

1

We are the heirs of the Natural Law philosophers and the theologians who polarized everything as good and bad, right and wrong, whereas the very nature of science on which our industrial society is based is that conclusions are *always* conditional — conditioned by time, place, situation, observer, as well as by the possibility that new evidence may result in new conclusions.[3] From laboratory experiment we are informed: "Actually . . . cleverness, or worth themselves are largely a function of *who makes the statements and to whom they are made.*"[4]

This tendency to polarize originates in our early acculturation. In childhood we relate to members of the family and learn that we must "be on one side or the other." [5]

We are inclined to accept those who accept us and reject those who reject us,[6] and, similarly, to accept the ideas of those who accept us, *i.e.,* the "good" people, and reject the ideas of those who reject us, *i.e.,* the "bad" people. For example, we tend to believe the man who hits us is in the wrong; and the man we hit did the wrong thing, not we. He is the "bad" one. It was the other fellow who drove negligently and was responsible for the accident. ". . . This tendency to regress to simple categories of perception is especially strong under conditions of emotional stress and external threat. Witness our readiness in times of war to exalt the virtues of our own side and to see the enemy as thoroughly evil." [7] On the other hand, as George Eliot said in *Middlemarch,* "The text, whether of prophet or poet, expands for whatever we can put into it, and even his bad grammar is sublime."

Hugo Münsterberg, who dramatized in his classes the inaccuracies of observation of events occurring in the room, was one of the first scholars to point out the discrepancies between evidence of the senses and evidence of the law. Although

---

[3] Lundberg, *Conflicting Orientation in Law and National Policy,* in TAYLOR, LIFE, LANGUAGE, LAW 168 (1957).

[4] Horwitz, Lyons & Perlmutter, *Induction of Forces in Discussion Groups,* 4, No. 1 HUMAN RELATIONS 57, 74 (1951).

[5] SAUL, THE HOSTILE MIND 130-31 (1956).

[6] Brown, *Models of Attitude Change,* in BROWN, GALANTIER, HESS & MANDLER, 1 NEW DIRECTIONS IN PSYCHOLOGY 38-39 (1962).

[7] Bronfenbrenner, *The Mirror Image in Soviet-American Relations, A Social Psychologist's Report,* 17, No. 3 J. SOCIAL ISSUES 45-56 (1961).

social-psychology has developed and modified many of his ideas, his genius stands out in its application of experimental psychology to the courtroom. In his *On the Witness Stand,* first published in 1908, he described discrepancies between perception and recall as psychological processes and the assumptions of the courtroom regarding them. He also pointed out some of the deficiencies in trial procedure from the viewpoint of psychology.[8] Some of his experiments are well known. They are repeated in classrooms and frequently referred to by lawyers. Their validity has not been questioned, but their application to the law has not been attempted. It is as though lawyers admitted the contradiction between psychology and traditional legal practices and held up their hands in despair at the thought of experimenting to eliminate them, to make possible testimony that is more reliable.

In the 1920's, in the course of an intellectual quest for a truth that could be discovered experientially, some consideration was given to the relationship between psychological findings and the rules of evidence. A few studies were presented as observations on the laws of evidence under the auspices of Robert Hutchins and Donald Slesinger at Yale and Mortimer Adler and Jerome Michael at Columbia, but these were essentially exploratory. "By careful use of [the scientists'] . . . proved results in these and other fields," Hutchins and Slesinger wrote, "we may yet build a law of evidence more closely related to the facts of human behavior." [9]

It is the purpose of this book to carry this line of thought further in the light of more recent studies by social-psychologists. First will be considered the conflict between the law of evidence and empirical research and the need to press further research to devise means to gain greater accuracy in evidence on which to determine responsibility, damages, and guilt. Secondly, there will be discussion of the trial process and its effects on the search for reality.

---

[8] MÜNSTERBERG, ON THE WITNESS STAND: ESSAYS ON PSYCHOLOGY AND CRIME 15-36, 50 (1923) and PSYCHOLOGY: GENERAL AND APPLIED ch. 30 (1915).

[9] Hutchins & Slesinger, *Some Observations on the Law of Evidence — Memory,* 41 HARV. L. REV. 860, 873 (1928).

CHAPTER I

PSYCHOLOGY AND EVIDENCE

"Have sight and hearing truth in them?
Are they not, as the poets are always
telling us, inaccurate witnesses?"
Socrates [10]

I. The Setting

The atmosphere of the courtroom is not normally such that one could expect to find the truth of a situation; at best one finds only a rough approximation. The courtroom is not a laboratory. As one lawyer addressing others concluded: "I don't have to tell you that a law suit is not a disinterested investigation but a bitter adversary duel." [11]

Francis Wellman, speaking of cross-examination, says: "It is a mental duel between counsel and witness." [12] He continues: "It is the love of combat which every man possesses that fastens the attention of the jury upon the progress of the trial." [13] He might have added that most cases are so dull in their succession of witnesses and documents that only the element of combat they contain can hold the attention of judge and jury.

The Supreme Court, sitting above the clamor of the trial courts among its colonnades on Capitol Hill, whose opinions are interpreted by the Delphic Oracles on the benches of inferior courts, has told us: "The adversary system of trial is hardly an end in itself; it is not yet a poker game in which players enjoy an absolute right always to conceal their cards until played." [14]

---

[10] Phaedo, Sir R. W. Livingston, transl. (1938).
[11] Gair, *The Dynamics of a Negligence Trial,* 19 N.Y. COUNTY LAW. A.B. BULL. 110, 114 (1962).
[12] WELLMEN, THE ART OF CROSS-EXAMINATION 8 (1936).
[13] *Id.* at 14.
[14] *Williams v. Florida,* 399 U.S. 78, 81, 90 S.Ct. 1893, 1896 (1970).

While it is true that the rigidities of early Anglo-American pleadings have been relaxed and that pre-trial discovery proceedings,[15] bills of particular and interrogatories have narrowed issues and lessened surprise, and there may be no absolute right to conceal cards, nevertheless, the poker game remains a valid description of a hotly contested trial. It is a game in which some cards are still concealed and bluff remains an integral part.

Despite the ethical pronouncements of the Supreme Court and Bar Associations, the psychology of the trial tends to be a games theory, a win-lose theory rather than an attempt by the parties and their counsel to find fact. McCarty illustrates this in his description of a common practice in preparing witnesses to testify:

> "It is very important in interviewing witnesses that the first impression be favorable. This is where suggestion comes in. Do you ask the witness what happened and let him tell the story? Not if you are experienced and know the psychology of approach. You start out and tell him what happened, giving your client's story and then go back and go over it item by item and have the witness verify it. In this way his memory will be refreshed from your standpoint and he will be more apt to make a good witness for your client." [16]

In important cases the impartial objectives of the courtroom are further contaminated by the public drama stimulated by the mass media. The famous *Hall-Mills* case was full of testimony from witnesses whose perception and knowledge of the case was evidently stimulated by the newspaper accounts and the notoriety involved.[17]

The moves and counter-moves of attorneys "pursuant to a complex system of rules, each trying to gain advantage for its cause," and the stimulant of publicity which affected court and counsel, are revealed by the story of the trial of Jack Ruby. Ruby killed Oswald, the assassin of President Kennedy, while an estimated sixty million watched at their television sets. In the Ruby

---

[15] How discovery proceedings may be abused, impede litigation and interfere with privacy, see N.Y. Times, June 28, 1978, p. A15.

[16] PSYCHOLOGY AND THE LAW 213 (1960).

[17] KUNSTLER, THE MINISTER AND THE CHOIR SINGER (1964).

trial everything was distorted and almost every distortion was in full view of millions of people.[18]

Dean Wigmore would have us distinguish between " 'contentiousness,' which is a fault of behavior, and 'contentious procedure,' which merely denotes the scientific fact that our system relies upon *the parties, not the judge,* to search for evidence and to present it, each in rivalry with the other. The former may be merely a remediable abuse, separable from the system itself; the latter may be a sound principle." [19] The question arises as to the criteria by which soundness is measured. Is a field dominated by hostility, for example, one in which objective data can reasonably be procured?

At times, seemingly respectable attorneys will, to win a case, indulge in trickery though it may mean the very life of a defendant. A dramatic example of this occurred in the cross-examination of a witness and the summation by the assistant district attorney in the celebrated murder trial of Nan Patterson.[20] Clever cross-examination intended as a means to justice became an end in itself and the "mental duel" became a self-sufficing exercise though the executioner awaited the conclusion.

This courtroom combat, this "adversary duel," is a sublimation of more direct forms of hostile aggression in primitive societies, such as blood feuds and individual or clan acts of revenge. It is a game we play within rules called laws of jurisdiction and of evidence, laws criminal and civil. As a sublimation of direct action this serves a useful social purpose, for the element of competition and the release of hostility are essential. But the combat, the duel, the game are certainly not the best ways to discover truth, nor are they well calculated to arrive at just compensation or fitting penalties.

Seeking the truth, fact, or reality in this unscientific atmosphere, the court hears evidence. We are not so much concerned here with the rules of evidence themselves as with the quality or value of the evidence offered under the rules. Indeed, the artificiality of many

---

[18] KAPLAN & WALTZ, THE TRIAL OF JACK RUBY 9 (1965).
[19] 1 WIGMORE, EVIDENCE § 8c, at 284-85 (3d ed. 1940).
[20] LEVY, THE NAN PATTERSON CASE ch. 24 (1959); and see examples of legitimatized tricks of the trade by the district attorney in the trial of Jack Ruby, KAPLAN & WALTZ, *op. cit. supra* note 18, at 106-08, 155.

of the rules of evidence has led to an excessive focus on the means at the expense of the end. Dean Wigmore notes that the rules have become more rationalized in theory but less rationally applied toward "the ascertainment of truth . . . fought over with irrelevant snarling and yapping." [21]

Nor are we primarily concerned with the problem of perjured testimony. When there is a conflict in evidence the court attempts to discover which side is telling the truth, whereas frequently the question is: Is either side telling the truth? For "evidence itself is far less trustworthy than the public usually realizes. . . . People as a rule do not reflect upon their meager opportunities for observing facts, and rarely suspect the frailty of their own powers of observation. They come to court, if summoned as witnesses, prepared to tell what they think they know; and in the beginning they resent an attack upon their story as they would upon their integrity." [22]

Mr. Justice Cardozo suggests that "As political economy has its economic man, so jurisprudence has its reasonable man, its negligent man," etc. The law, he tells us, "is no stranger to the philosophy of the 'As If.' It has built up many of its doctrines by make-believe that things are other than they are." [23]

Because law has not developed its own experimental discipline, it has the responsibility to test its "make-believe" doctrine by whatever scientific methods are available and adjust those doctrines insofar as it can to reality. If the law cannot achieve this within the traditions of the courtroom, then it would seem that substitute legal institutions should be provided whenever they are better suited to reality. Whenever the "As If" can be replaced by the "Is," the make-believe should give way.

II. The Make-Believe of Evidence

Let us take a look at some of the principal "As Ifs" related to evidence. Except in commercial cases, the greater part of evidence

---

[21] Wigmore, *Jury-Trial Rules of Evidence in the Next Century,* in LAW: A CENTURY OF PROGRESS 1835-1935, at 347 (Reppy ed. 1937).

[22] WELLMAN, *op. cit. supra* note 12, at 7, 10.

[23] CARDOZO, THE PARADOXES OF LEGAL SCIENCE 33-34 (1928), referring to VAIHINGER, DIE PHILOSOPHIE DES ALS OB [THE PHILOSOPHY OF THE "AS IF"] (Ogden transl. 1935).

introduced into the courts is testimony of what the eyewitness saw, what the hearer heard and what the witness remembers of occurrences, sometimes occurrences years distant in time. Implicit, if not always explicit, is the assumption that witnesses can see accurately, hear accurately, and recall accurately. This assumption which is the keystone "As If" of the law of evidence, is in fact contradicted by the findings of psychological science.

There are many points between the occurrence and the verdict at which the incident in dispute may be distorted, intentionally or not. The areas in which the witness might unwittingly distort that which happens may be divided into three categories: [24] (A) *Perception*, including (1) the limitations on the range and acuteness of human sense perception and (2) the way events are interpreted and significances assigned to them (*i.e.*, the determination of sense perception) by a person's idiosyncratic needs, moods, and emotions; (B) *Recollection*, the time lapse between the accident and its recounting, during which other influences on the observer permit the image of the incident to be altered; and (C) *Articulation*, the basic problem of communication, whereby the same words are used with different meanings by different persons. This indication of the imperfections in testimony of events concerns the refractions of the truth that relate to the witness vis-á-vis the event; comparable distortions occur during the transaction between the witness and the jurors, and among the jurors when they convene to discuss the testimony in the jury room.

A. PERCEPTION

1. RANGE AND ACUTENESS.

Modern social science has learned much about each of these areas, and especially in the category of sense perception psychologists stress the disparity between even the simplest stimulus, *i.e.*, object or event, and the perception of it. "[T]here are no concrete absolutes in perception: instead, what is perceived may roughly be described as a series of functional probabilities." [25]

---

[24] Compare Thomas, *Cross-Examination of Witnesses*, in TORT AND MEDICAL YEARBOOK 57, 72 (Averbach & Belli ed. 1961).

[25] Kilpatrick & Cantril, *The Constancies in Social Perception*, in EXPLORATIONS IN TRANSACTIONAL PSYCHOLOGY 354-65, at 357 (Kilpatrick ed. 1961).

"Apparently," notes Kilpatrick, "the correspondence between percept and object is never absolute. Instead, perception is of functional probabilities, of constructs which emerge from the consequences of past action and serve as directives for furthering the purposes of the organism through action. 'Percept' and 'object' are but two abstracted aspects of this total process and correspondence between the two is simply a function of their being part and parcel of the same thing." [26]

What this means to the layman is that all of the physical aspects of our environment vary to each individual in terms of his own experiences. What you and I see when two cars proceed down a street and collide is not the identical cars, streets, and collisions, but cars, streets, and collisions fashioned from our respective experiences with them. Take another example. We see a young woman with two small children and, based on experience and probability, we assume she is their mother. If we have some question about our judgment we look for a wedding ring or try to hear their conversation to reinforce our conclusion.

Psychology views the individual, his surroundings, his past, and his future, as integrated into a continuous flow of data back and forth, through experience and through stimuli to the senses. It treats perception itself as the individual's awareness of a "thing" or "happening" conditioned by his similar experiences in the past and designed to direct his behavior in the future to be consistent with what he already knows. To these "things" or "happenings" one assigns out of his arsenal of experience significances, meanings, and values.

It is the premise of the transactional psychologists that man's basic drive is toward security, not only in the emotional sense but in terms of being in harmony with his environment. The greater the constancy of that environment, the higher the degree of security that it will yield. Change of environment requires a re-evaluation of the external world so that the individual, trying to regain his security, can realign himself with those persons or things or happenings external to him. Man's perceptions are guided by this need to maintain psychological equilibrium. To insure a predictable environment, perception can magnify or diminish the

---

[26] *Id.* at 4.

importance of certain information, and actually distort quality and size.[27]

Some simple demonstrations of how our sense perceptions are governed by what we already know about the world around us have been produced by artificially manipulating "cues" to perceptions such as size, distance, brightness, and other physical properties. Such perceptions are commonly involved in negligence cases and frequently in other ligitation. It may be startling to many of us to learn that a cue to a perception of distance, for example, is a witness's prior experience with the size of objects in the field of vision. An experiment indicating this involves showing playing cards of different sizes to an observer in a darkened room where he has no points of reference for what he sees. When an observer sees, in these circumstances, a playing card that is twice the size of the conventional playing card with which his past experience has familiarized him, he is so conditioned by that past experience that he expects the card to be of the same size as those to which he is accustomed. He therefore will assume that it is in fact twice as close, rather than that it is twice as large. These demonstrations [28] have convinced researchers that the perception of *where* a thing is depends on perceptions of *what* a thing is and on *when* it is perceived.

Thus, in even the simplest perceptual process, the mind takes over and adjusts what the senses report to the past perceptual experience in order to maintain that stability of environment on which the human organism flourishes. Similar experiments with cigarette packs, magazines, and other objects of standard size have reinforced this finding that size and distance are experientially related, and that size is the dominant "cue" that will govern the readjustment of the perception of other characteristics. The strength of size as a cue has been reinforced by its constancy within experience, for size is a more constant attribute of the object itself, and less subject to variation than other perceived characteristics such as distance, brightness, color, and consistency. A further demonstration of the role of experience in governing these perceptions is reported by Ames and Ittelson, who found that

---

[27] Stagner, *Personality Dynamics and Social Conflict,* 17, No. 3 J. SOCIAL ISSUES 28, 33 (1961).

[28] Kilpatrick & Cantril, *op. cit. supra* note 25, at 36.

in the experiment with playing cards of various sizes, only young observers, presumably less rigidly conditioned by past experience because such experience was more limited, could accommodate to changes in the size of the cards.[29]

When we do not have experiential information about size, we deduce size from whatever other strong cues are available. A common example is the "moon illusion." The moon looks larger on the horizon than at the zenith because on the horizon it is seen in relation to things on the landscape. It is measured against things of known size at distances which we have experienced. This is not so when the moon is "a disembodied body" overhead.[30] Rock and Kaufman include a picture showing a black rectangle in the foreground and another, of the same size, on the horizon. The effect of distance on size is such that the rectangle on the horizon seems larger than the other, although they are exactly the same in size. This effect is greatly increased with a three-dimensional scene where the impression of depth is stronger. The reason for this is that the related stimuli "that normally accompany changes in distance may be registered by the brain and automatically affect size perception without conscious recognition of this effect on the part of the observer." [31]

---

[29] See Ames, Jr. & Ittelson, *Accommodation, Convergence, and Apparent Distance,* in EXPLORATIONS IN TRANSACTIONAL PSYCHOLOGY 99, 118 (Kilpatrick ed. 1961).

[30] Kaufman & Rock, *The Moon Illusion,* 136, No. 3521 SCIENCE 1023.

[31] *Id.* No. 3520, at 961 n.1.

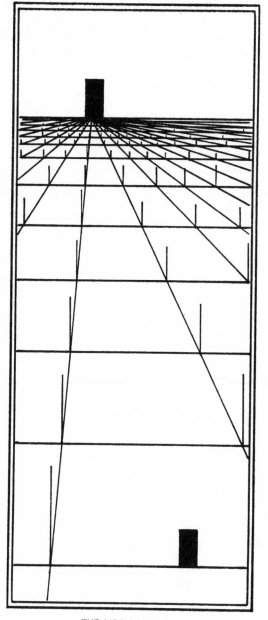

THE MOON ILLUSION

Reproduced by permission from Science Magazine.

These scientific explorations of the most elementary perceptions have been carried from the laboratory test situation to the more sophisticated occurrences of daily life, and applied to *aural* as well as visual perception.[32] Witnesses testify to what they heard as well as to what they saw. What do they hear? Kilpatrick reports that the novel sound of an oncoming tornado was conformed to past experience by many hearers who accepted it as the sound of an oncoming train; thus perceptual similarities are converted by the observer into identities in order to maintain the stability of his environment and thus his harmony with it.

As Thucydides suggested, we do something very similar when we *recall* spoken words. We reconstruct conversations "of course adhering as closely as possible to the general sense of what was really said." [33] None of us hears all the words or other sounds that occur in our presence. Many of us are deaf to certain tones and we miss the words or syllables in that tonal range, or we have some other diminution in hearing. What we do to adjust to such phenomena in normal conversation, or in listening to lecturers or arguments, is to fill in blanks as we believe the speaker might have meant them. We put together what we have heard with what we sense we might have missed in order to make a whole which is acceptable to us, thereby conforming our perceptions to our expectations. Obviously, this provides an opportunity to realize our expectations, to engage in wishful thinking. Thus a witness can in good honor swear to the truth of what he did not hear, to a damaging statement which a party never made or perhaps made in terms that were in reality not damaging to him.

It is difficult to resist the temptation at times to cite fiction rather than research to illustrate psychological phenomena. The author cannot resist referring to the song of Alice's friend the Knight when she went *Through the Looking Glass* to illustrate selective listening. The Knight described questioning an aged, aged man "A-sitting on a gate" concerning his age and how he lived. The

---

[32] Kilpatrick, *Perception in Critical Situations,* in EXPLORATIONS IN TRANSACTIONAL PSYCHOLOGY 316-20 (Kilpatrick ed. 1961).

[33] THUCYDIDES, COMPLETE WRITINGS, *op. cit. supra* note 1.

aged man made several attempts to answer, but the Knight
admitted:

> ". . . his answer trickled through my head Like
> water through a sieve."

The Knight meanwhile was thinking of other things, until the aged,
aged man ending by saying:

> "And very gladly will I drink
> To your Honor's noble health."

This last point made a pleasing impression on the Knight.[34] He
could hear it. When we ask questions, frequently we don't listen
to the answer, except when it is something that we want to hear,
something that gives us support.

This selective process and inventive reconstruction of
conversations has been recognized in law by "the hearsay rule."
The law has long attempted to avoid testimony of hearsay that
cannot be balanced by rebuttal. But even when the testimony of
a witness can be modified or refuted by another witness, both
reports are inevitably selective and inventive. Rumor is a form of
hearsay and as such is not admitted in evidence (except in such
instances as character testimony) because the law recognizes that
it is imprecise, selective, and secondhand. Rumor does, however,
affect the processes of perception and recall because it is an
experience. For, by the process already described, in order to
maintain harmony with his environment, one who hears a rumor
will often tend to accredit it to his own perception.

The gap created by a lack of knowledge or perception, of some
fact that we deem necessary to reach a conclusion, will tend to
create in us a sense of incongruity with respect to the remaining
data. Therefore, in order to dispel this incongruity, we try to fill
the gap by obtaining further data. But the jury cannot do this once
they are in the jury room, except perhaps by having a portion of
the testimony read to them. This, however, may not meet their
needs. What happens then is what happens frequently in other
situations. The gap may be filled in with rumor. Frequently this

---

[34] CARROLL, ALICE'S ADVENTURES IN WONDERLAND and THROUGH THE LOOKING
GLASS 177, 180 (Macmillan & Co. ed. 1930).

gap in knowledge arouses suspicion and jurymen may create their own rumor or even gossip. This rumor can be of such a character as will justify some fear or stress that the jurors may have. It may act to justify either hostile or affirmative feelings they have against one of the parties, witnesses, or attorneys.[35]

We sometimes read drama into perception. For example, when two moving dots are shown on a screen, the larger behind the smaller, the larger is perceived as "chasing" the smaller. But when the larger is shown in front, it is generally seen as "leading." [36] The perception reflects some of our earliest childhood experiences. What we define as "good" or "bad" reflects in our perception of such matters as the facial expression of men on a picket line. To the management it appears "threatening," to labor "determined." [37]

An automobile accident is an exceedingly complex and sudden occurrence taking less than ten seconds.[38] No matter how accurately it is observed, it cannot be perceived in an exact manner by any witness. In other words, not only is eyewitness testimony of such an occurrence necessarily inaccurate; it is also in essential points incomplete.

In many tort and criminal cases *duration of events* is an important factor. Witnesses are asked to testify as to the interval between an occurrence and the action of a party or some third person. Experiments have demonstrated that we do not judge the passage of time accurately, and that "visual durations that were the same as auditory durations were judged shorter," [39] by about twenty percent.[40]

---

[35] FESTINGER, A THEORY OF COGNITIVE DISSONANCE 235-43 (1957).

[36] Heider & Simmel, *An Experimental Study of Apparent Behavior,* 57 AMERICAN J. PSYCHOLOGY 243, 254 (1944).

[37] OSGOOD, GRADUATED RECIPROCATION IN TENSION-REDUCTION 22 (n.d.).

[38] NORMAN, ROAD TRAFFIC ACCIDENTS (1962).

[39] Goldstone, Bordman & Lhamon, *Intersensory Comparisons of Temporal Judgments,* 57 J. EXPERIMENTAL PSYCHOLOGY 243-48 (1959).

[40] Behar & Bevar, *The Perceived Duration of Auditory and Visual Intervals: Cross Model Comparison and Interaction,* 74 AMERICAN J. PSYCHOLOGY 17-26 (1961).

Danger and stress also affect the estimate of time and distance. This overestimate tends to increase as danger increases. As laymen we are accustomed to the concept that in emergencies time seems endless, but as lawyers we ignore the reality that with increasing danger "space and time stretch," [41] and so accept the validity of a party's testimony that the car was a hundred yards away when he stepped off the curb, or the statement of a car driver as to when he sounded his horn. Not only the duration, but the *sequence* of events may be difficult to perceive. This too may be an important issue of fact, as when the question in an assault case is who struck first, or in a matrimonial proceeding, who spoke first.[42]

The law of evidence takes a contrary view concerning the impact of stress. The *res gestae* rule governing the admission of spontaneous explanations by a participant in an event is justified on the theory that the impact of intensity, the "stress of nervous excitement" as Dean Wigmore calls it, will make for "a spontaneous and sincere response...." [43] That is, legal theory maintains that in the "stress of nervous excitement" the witness does not consciously try to make self-serving declarations as to his perceptions, and therefore his statements are more reliable. It ignores, however, the distorting impact of trauma on the capacity to perceive.

The importance of judging distance when observing an automobile accident is obvious. Yet if *distance perception* is merely a secondary or derivative perception, as has been shown, then any witness's report of distance must be subject to so many other conditions that it may be unreliable. Another essential of any eyewitness report of an automobile accident is perception of motion, and this too has been demonstrated to be a secondary, or

---

[41] Langer, Wapner & Werner, *The Effect of Danger upon the Experience of Time,* 74 AMERICAN J. PSYCHOLOGY 94-97 (1961).

[42] Doehring, *Accuracy and Consistency of Time-Estimation by Four Methods of Reproduction,* 74 AMERICAN J. PSYCHOLOGY 27 et seq. (1961) (describing experiments on individual's ability to judge time); and see ch. III.

[43] 6 WIGMORE, EVIDENCE § 1747, at 135 (3d ed. 1940).

derivative, characteristic, dependent upon size, apparent distance, lighting, angle of vision, and the known attributes of the object perceived in motion.[44]

With respect to relative size, Gardner notes that we tend to overestimate the length of verticals, and to exaggerate the difference if one average-sized person is surrounded by many exceptionally short or tall ones, and find that the one person is the exception and the others are the average.[45]

In view of the frequent use of *photographs,* a word about them is relevant. Wide angle lenses will tend to make each item smaller and spread out the picture so that objects appear further from each other, both horizontally and in depth, than they would to the normal eye. The reverse is true when telephoto lenses are used. Different filters and film emulsions, whether black and white or color, vary the color values on prints and transparencies. The angle or elevation from which a picture is taken can affect truthful rendition and magnify or minimize obstructions. It is found that in some situations foreground items on a photographic print look nearer on the left than on the right. Items in the background do not follow this rule.[46]

Comparative brightness may indicate movement. Since brightness has some of the constant characteristics of size and will dominate those "cues" of lesser constancy, when the strength of a pinpoint of light is varied in a darkened room the observer concludes that the point is moving, toward him when it becomes brighter, away when it becomes dimmer.[47] Brightness may also be taken as a cue to distance. Early astronomers, for example, assumed that the brightest stars were certainly closest to the

---

[44] Kilpatrick & Ittelson, *The Perception of Movement,* in EXPLORATIONS IN TRANSACTIONAL PSYCHOLOGY 58-68 (Kilpatrick ed. 1961).

[45] Gardner, *The Perception and Memory of Witnesses,* 18 CORNELL L.Q. 391-98 (1933).

[46] Bartley & DeHardt, *A Further Factor in Determining Nearness as a Function of Lateral Orientation in Pictures,* 50 J. PSYCHOLOGY 53-57 (1960); Bartley & DeHardt, *Phenomenal Distance in Scenes with Independent Manipulation of Major and Minor Items, id.* at 315.

[47] Kilpatrick & Ittelson, *supra* note 44.

earth. Since there was no experiential information about the actual size of a star, its brightness was taken as an indication of its distance from the observer.

Motion, in terms of *direction and velocity,* has also been found to be governed largely by cues of size and overlay, overlay being the apparent sequence of objects in space as related to the observer, indicated by what commonly appears to be the obstructed perception of one object by another object seemingly nearer to the observer. This has been demonstrated by the famous experiments with the "rotating trapezoid," a two-dimensional representation of what appears to be a window frame in perspective. The perceptual conflicts that arise when the "frame" is rotated while an object moves on a straight line through one of the "panes" create a dissonance in perceptions that most observers resolve by rationalizing the motion. In this case the overlay produced by the object (in these experiments a playing card) and the rotating trapezoid conflicted with and dominated the constant size, speed, and direction of the object, leading to the rationalization by the observer that the size, speed, and direction of the object had been varied during the experiment.[48]

But as Ames, who developed this rotating trapezoid, reported, certain characteristics of it will be seen by all observers, and others will vary with the viewer's locus in time and space. For example, the experience of all viewers was so strong in terms of perspective that they were unable to accept the rotation of the trapezoid because that would have placed the side of the "window" that should have been farther away nearer to them. They therefore observed the rotating motion as an oscillation, even when a cube was attached to the trapezoid to indicate its actual motion by creating overlay. Furthermore, when the trapezoid was at rest, if the *observer* moved slightly to the right or left the trapezoid appeared to be in motion.

Observation of velocity is especially difficult, and practically

---

[48] Kilpatrick & Ittelson, *supra* note 44; also Ames, *The Rotating Trapezoid: Description of Phenomena,* in EXPLORATIONS IN TRANSACTIONAL PSYCHOLOGY 222 (Kilpatrick ed. 1961).

every automobile accident case produces testimonial variations of from five to twenty-five percent as to speed. Extensive experience in driving or watching moving vehicles will increase the observer's likelihood of accuracy. In general, the perception of the rate of tangential motion is easier to gauge than motion toward or away from the viewer.[49] A test among air force personnel found that even among observers who knew in advance that they were to estimate the speed of a moving car the guesses ranged from ten to fifty miles per hour, even though the car was in fact going at only twelve miles per hour.[50] Other tests mentioned in the same report show that a car's color, body style, and noise influence the witness's estimate of speed. Parenthetically, the body size and style of a car may relate to biases in the observer, some people apparently being biased against large cars, others against small ones or convertibles. Weight is a frequent issue in tort and criminal cases. It appears that color influences perception of weight as well as estimates of speed, apparent brightness being a major cue to estimates of weight.[51]

Just as experience gives rise to expectations that are used to fill the gaps in hearing, so experience and expectation fill blanks in perceptions of motion. We expect that "movement will occur in the direction in which previous presentation [or the same or a similar situation] was perceived to move." [52] This finding is particularly applicable to converging traffic and the movements of persons at the scene of an occurrence involved in litigation.

Filling gaps in perception is a betting process. We select what we believe will be harmonious with those elements we have perceived and repress those that will create conflicts for us. The elements that we choose or repress will depend on what bet,[53] or what selection, we make as the likeliest explanation for what we

---

[49] Gardner, *supra* note 45.

[50] 3, No. 12 AMERICAN SOCIETY FOR PUBLIC ADMINISTRATION BULL. 4 (1959).

[51] Payne, Jr., *Apparent Weight as a Function of Color*, 71 AMERICAN J. PSYCHOLOGY 725-30 (1958). See also Payne, Jr., *Apparent Weight as a Function of Hue*, 74 *id.* (1961), at 104.

[52] Krampen & Toch, *The Determination of Perceived Movement Direction*, 50 J. PSYCHOLOGY 271-77 (1960).

[53] See Ittelson, *The Constancies of Visual Perception*, in EXPLORATIONS IN TRANSACTIONAL PSYCHOLOGY 339-51 (Kilpatrick ed. 1961).

see; and that bet will, of course, be conditioned by past experience in similar situations.

The rotating trapezoid has been used in many ingenious ways to demonstrate our need to reconcile conflicts in what we think we see with what we know from experience. One of the most compelling demonstrations shows how easy it is to condition the observer's assumptions, or rationalizations, that perceptual conflicts will necessitate. Each observer is handed a steel cylinder to feel and return to the experimenter who is to place it perpendicular to the rotating trapezoid within one of the "panes." This process is then repeated with a rubber cylinder, and the viewer is asked to describe the motion he has observed. More than half of the observers saw a difference in the motion in the two situations, with most reporting some lengthening or cutting through of the "window" by the first cylinder (presumed to be steel) and some bending of the second cylinder (presumed to be rubber) as it and the trapezoid rotated. In fact, the experimenter had inserted a plastic cylinder in both cases, but the suggestion created by the known, experienced characteristics of steel and rubber respectively justified for the viewer two different reconciliations of the apparent disparity in motion perceived. Kilpatrick describes this necessary reconciliation as the product of the observer's repression of the element that he believes to have created the conflict.[54]

This "betting" process as an element in perception has been described by Ittelson as "the product of the continual recoding of the relatedness of things as defined by action . . . the apprehension of *probable* significance." [55] This is further indicated by Toch's finding that all observers who perceived objects briefly flashed on a slide to be bombs believed that they saw the objects depicted as falling. Those who properly identified vertical airplanes, nose up, saw them as soaring upward.[56]

---

[54] Kilpatrick, *Assumptions and Perceptions: Three Experiments, id.* at 257, 276-87.

[55] Ittelson, *supra* note 53.

[56] See Krampen & Toch, *supra* note 52.

At this point we might also notice a cue that is a variation on overlay-perspective. That we tend to construct the third dimension of a special relationship between two objects on the basis of their two-dimensional relationship is especially apparent in experiments with parallel vertical lines; two lines of different lengths, the bottom of the shorter one lower than the bottom of the longer one, will be perceived as lines of different sizes at the same distance from the viewer. But, if the midpoints of the two are at the same level, then they will appear to be the same size but at a different distance from the observer. In the latter case, the assumption of same size and different distance is reinforced by adding a third parallel line between the two and intermediate in size and space.[57] This process by which we take a chance on the probable significance of perception can be treated also in terms of expectation calling for reinforcement or release of some tension.[58]

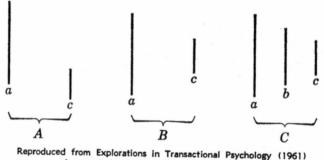

Three-dimensional or space perception is not a simple view of a scene. When, for example, "an observer moves his head or body while looking at some particular object in space, the retinal image of that scene is displaced across the retinal surface. The amount of displacement is again proportional to the relative distance of each object to the point of fixation." [59]

---

[57] Kilpatrick, *The Nature of Perception: Some Visual Demonstrations, op. cit. supra* note 25, at 36, 44.

[58] MURPHY, PERSONALITY 89 (1947).

[59] Haber, *Visual Perception,* ANN. REV. OF PSYCHOLOGY, 29:31, 33 (Rosenzweig & Porter eds. 1978). This is an interesting though extremely technical review of research and theory of three-dimensional perception, among other things.

Perception in considerable part occurs while the head or body or both are in motion. "Such motion produces continuous transformation of the retinal image, not discrete or separate images." [60]

Such transformations include an overlap as in a motion picture. "Retinal images cannot be a two-dimensional picture from which we infer a three-dimensional scene. Rather, the visual system takes information from the succession of retinal images and uses that succession to construct a single panoramic three-dimensional view." [61] It is something like the process of surveying. This would account in part for different perceptions of witnesses with respect to distance and the relationships of persons and objects in space.

When to Believe is to See.

Let us consider expectation the readiness for reinforcement of some need. Need is a tension in a human system and at the same time a motive or drive for some conscious or unconscious behavior. What one's expectation or readiness for reinforcement in a particular instance will be relates to: (1) his need to be reinforced; (2) his estimate of the "probability of occurrence of [a possible] . . . outcome"; and (3) his estimate of the ". . . desirability of [the] outcome." [62] What this means in terms of motivation of parties to a proceeding and witnesses will be discussed later.[63] At this point it is only necessary to say that expectation, such readiness for reinforcement, determines the "bet" made to explain what has been seen or heard and offered as testimony. Thus if we have a need, a motive, to identify the man who committed the theft, and the man the police show us is sufficiently similar in appearance to be the probable thief, and we believe it desirable to identify the thief, we tend to have a readiness to be reinforced in our identification by the very fact that the police show us such a man in the lineup. Similarly our belief that we crossed the intersection

---

[60] Op. cit. 37.
[61] Op. cit. 38.
[62] STOGDILL, INDIVIDUAL BEHAVIOR AND GROUP ACHIEVEMENT 63 (1959).
[63] See text, pp.   infra.
[63] See text, pp. 137-39 infra.

while the light was green is supported by the expectation that we could not have gone against a red light because our experience tells us that we always stop on red.

The compelling force of experience upon the observer is explained psychologically in terms of the past successes in similar perception. This is an essentially pragmatic process, *i.e.,* if in the past this particular assumption has been validated by action, then it has been tested, it "works," and it should remain as at least a working hypothesis until some strong challenge to it is presented that will dictate the application of a different set of experiences. In this way man adjusts to his environment, clinging to that which is familiar and avoiding the unfamiliar by distorting it to fit into his previous perceptual framework. That is why the cues that are most often valid will dominate our perception, and those that are most variable will be subordinated.

It must be remembered in considering all of these "cues," or characteristics, that none of them is an attribute of the object itself independent of the beholder. All are derived from his total experience as brought to bear on a particular perception.

There is, as we have all experienced, no constancy to an individual's perception. The beholder, the witness, is not the identical person at different times. Some people who see well in daylight are aware that they do not see as clearly as others at dusk. Alcohol, drugs, exhaustion and emotional states such as anxiety affect perception.

Alcohol most particularly distorts perception. A large proportion of fatal motor vehicle accidents in the United States — in some years estimated as more than half — has been attributed to the use of alcohol. A publication of the New York Automobile Association states that alcohol limits the capacity of eyes to readapt to darkness after sudden flashes of light as from headlights of a passing car. Muscles that bring objects into focus are weakened; consequently markers, signs, other cars and pedestrians may become fuzzy. Depth of perception may become impaired; and the use of alcohol may create double vision or "tunnel vision" (as when a driver can see straight ahead but side vision, as at intersections, may be limited). Any of these phenomena may imperil drivers and others.[64]

Age may make a difference. Older persons, it has been found, are poorer judges spacially and have less accurate depth perception than middle aged persons. Perception of verticals may also differ at varying ages. This may mean that in a specific situation conflicting testimony is not caused by dishonesty, angle of view or other opportunity but is the result of chronological age of the various witnesses.[65] It has been found that menstruation and the premenstruum affect accident-proneness in women, probably because they are "responsible for a lowered judgment and slow reaction time."[66]

, The physiological condition of a witness is a relevant variable in determining the accuracy of his testimony. But, except in patent cases of drunkenness, drug addiction, hysteria, senility or youth, the trial process is not geared to evaluate the effects of physiological conditions on perception or the inconstancy of the capacity to perceive.

2. INTERPRETIVE JUDGMENTS AND SIGNIFICANCE.

We have discussed the inadequacies of perception common to all witnesses, and know that we are not free to interpret our perceptions without reference to our experience. Beyond this are the specific limitations such as color-blindness, nearsightedness or farsightedness, binocular or binaural imbalance, and other physiological conditions that may be unique to certain individuals. Just as perception is colored by the past, giving rise to the expectation that what has been will be repeated, so interpretation makes use of values that have demonstrated their validity in similar transactions, happenings, or events to give significance to the present. In other words, what we call interpretation is similar to the transactional nature of perception; perhaps it is a phase of it — a more conscious application of the same process by which we

---

[64] NEW YORK MOTORIST, December 1971.

[65] Chown & Heron, *Psychological Aspects of Aging in Man,* ANNUAL REVIEW OF PSYCHOLOGY 435-36 (1965).

[66] Dalton, *Menstruation and Accidents,* BRITISH MEDICAL J. 1425-26 (1960).

read into our perceptions of distance the cue offered by experience with the size of objects in the environment.

An example of interpretive judgment is found in Chapter III where people inferred that the woman in a picture was the mother of the baby because she had called out, "My baby!" She did nothing of the sort, but by assigning this significance to the scene the viewers attained a sense of constancy between what they had seen and what they expected. We do this daily off the witness stand as well as on it. Life would be difficult without such interpretive judgments. However, they make difficult an accurate determination of objective reality.

Interpretive judgments are conditioned not only by the observer's experience as a human being but as a *particular* human being. They are not only the product of limitations of sense perception that are common to all of us but also of the unique characteristics of the individual. The significances assigned to things and happenings are the result of values and of subjective attitudes that may be derived from age, race, nationality, sex, profession, religion — all lifetime experience.

Thus we move from the primarily physiological to the social level, and can observe here the same search for external constancy. Constancy has been defined as "the sum total of the estimates one has, based on past experience, of one's own capacities to deal with particular sets of impingements." [67] What this means is that the individual will generalize in order to establish unity of self and his society. He will see and establish patterns and tools for unifying various kinds of human behavior. "All of these significances that we build up about the self and about objects, people, events, symbols, or ideas fuse and orchestrate to give us our own unique reality world. Everything that has significances for us takes on its significances from our personal behavior center — in terms of our own purposes and our own actions," and, of course, expectations. "In other words, behavior is seen as ultimately aimed at a state categorized as 'equilibrium.' " [68]

---

[67] Kilpatrick & Cantril, *supra* note 25, at 357-58.

[68] Kilpatrick & Cantril, *id.* at 363; Toch & Hastorf, *Homeostasis in Psychology, A Review and Critique* 18, 1 PSYCHIATRY: JOURNAL FOR THE STUDY OF INTERPERSONAL PROCESSES 89, 90 (1955).

How interpretation is affected by and gives significance to an observer's commitment or loyalty is further illustrated by an experiment of Hastorf and Cantril. They showed students at Dartmouth and Princeton the official film of a particularly rough football game between the two colleges. The men of each college, ascribing different reasons for the claims of the other that the game was "rough and dirty," tended to see the infractions of the rules by their team very differently from the other school's men.[69]

The emphasis on the subjective is not meant to portray an exaggerated atomization of society in which each person is isolated by virtue of his unique nature. There is inevitably communication and the shared experience of a culture and of all the subcultural units that exist in a society. This emphasis is intended to demonstrate the unreliability of any single set of perceptions or interpretations, because they are a product of individual assumptions derived from experience. In the selection process involved we choose for our *attention* happenings related to our *intention*.[70]

Filling gaps in perception is a betting process. We select what we believe will be harmonious with those elements we have perceived and repress those that will create dissonance for us. *The elements that we choose or repress will depend on what bet,*[71] *or what selection, we make as the likeliest explanation for what we see; and that bet will, of course, be conditioned by past experience in similar situations.*[72]

Ideally, we should know what constitutes reality to each witness in order to evaluate his evidence. We should know the patterns of his selectivity, how his process of perception selects interpretations of objects and happenings and gives significances to them, and how in turn he interprets his perceptions to form a pattern that will give

---

[69] Hastorf & Cantril, *They Saw a Game: A Case Study,* 49, No. 1 J. ABNORMAL AND SOCIAL PSYCHOLOGY 129-34 (1954).

[70] CANTRIL, THE POLITICS OF DESPAIR 15-18 (1958).

[71] See Ittelson, *The Constancies of Visual Perception, op. cit. supra* note 53.

[72] The rotating trapezoid has been used in many ingenious ways to demonstrate our need to reconcile conflicts in what we think we see with what we know from experience. See text page 20. Kilpatrick, *Assumptions and Perceptions: Three Experiments,* in EXPLORATIONS IN TRANSACTIONAL PSYCHOLOGY, *op. cit. supra* note 54, at 257, 276-87.

him a needed constancy in his relation to the external world. This is impossible in the adversarial conflict of a courtroom.

B. RECOLLECTION

Considerable transformation of a happening and its initial perception occurs in recollection. (See Chapter III.) To demonstrate the fallibility of memory is one of the chief aims of the cross-examiner. Witnesses are historians and autobiographers; on the witness stand they are reconstructing past events. Many of them to the best of their ability attempt to do it honestly, but it is not strange to find the grossest imperfection even in the memory of an honest man. Not only may his hearing and his eyesight be defective, but all his recollections often are the product of an association of ideas, commingled and confused with rationalization, and "all his memory may be tinctured by a bias, sometimes subconscious, or colored by suggestion." [73] Not only do people vary in their native or trained capacities to recall what has occurred or what they have learned, but recollection is also affected by the circumstances in which the events have occurred, the learning taken place, or the story retold.

Observers commonly see more than they can report. It has been found that "at the time of exposure, and for a few tenths of a second thereafter, observers have two to three times as much information available as they can later report. The availability of this information declines rapidly. . . ." [74] The location of stimuli in the field of vision may affect the degree of an observer's recall as may the sequence with which certain items are reported, for memory is somewhat better with respect to the first items reported than those later reported. It would seem probable, however, that some of the "forgotten" material is suppressed, repressed, or subliminal and may be brought back to consciousness by new stimuli, such as direct or cross-examination or the testimony of

---

[73] STRYKER, THE ART OF ADVOCACY 94 (1954).

[74] Sperling, *The Information Available in Brief Visual Presentations,* 74, No. 11 PSYCHOLOGICAL MONOGRAPHS: GENERAL AND APPLIED 1, 26 (1960).

other witnesses.[75] (See Chapter IV.) By the time a witness testifies, the true order or recall usually has been lost.

Memory, too, is selective. Interrupted tasks may be remembered more frequently than those completed.[76] Individual personality, as one would expect, determines the nature of the selections made. People who are able to be decisive in making decisions "tend to recall more failures than successes." [77] The indecisive recall more successes than failures. For the latter, this serves the function of ego defense when they have been unable to act decisively.[78]

It has also been found that "an individual notes and remembers material which supports his social attitudes better than material which conflicts with these attitudes." The test here involved two statements, one very anti-Soviet, the other pro-Soviet. Two groups of students, one pro-Communist and one anti-Communist (in the early 1940's) read the two statements; the pro-Soviet selection was learned better and forgotten more slowly by the pro-Communist group; and the disparity was the reverse, and even greater, between the pro- and anti-Communists' retention of the anti-Soviet statement.[79] This again is a process of selection and "denial."

The time interval between the crime, the accident or other cause of action and the trial is usually several months, if not years. During that interval the witness's impression of the incident is subject to numerous stresses. Foremost is what we call the "curve of forgetting," a leveling-out process in which most of what

---

[75] *Id.* at 27. See also Schiff, *The Effects of Subliminal Stimuli on Guessing Accuracy,* 74 AMERICAN J. PSYCHOLOGY 54-60 (1961).

[76] Zeigarnik, *Das Behalten erledigter Handlugen,* 9 PSYCHOLOGISCHE FORSCHUNG 1-85 (1927), cited by Horowitz, *The Recall of Interrupted Group Tasks: An Experimental Study of Individual Motivation in Relation to Group Goals,* in CARTWRIGHT & ZANDER, GROUP DYNAMICS: RESEARCH AND THEORY 370-94 (2d ed. 1960).

[77] Horowitz, *Psychological Need as a Function of Social Environments,* in THE STATE OF THE SOCIAL SCIENCES 162-79 (White ed. 1956).

[78] See *id.* at 176-80.

[79] Levine & Murphy, *The Learning and Forgetting of Controversial Material,* in READINGS IN SOCIAL PSYCHOLOGY 94-101 (Maccoby, Newcomb & Hartley 3d ed. 1958). See also Bartlett, *Social Factors in Recall,* in *id.* at 47, 53.

happens is forgotten within a matter of hours or days.[80] (See Chapter III.)

The intensity of the impression is also governed by its emotional impact. For example, the ordinary occurrence is less memorable than the unusual; it is essentially neutral because it makes no new demand upon the perceptual adjustments an observer makes to incorporate the occurrence in his framework of experience.[81]

We know too little about the relation of stress to recollection to form a working principle. However, it seems that under social stress those percepts which are most familiar are remembered best. "Whenever strong, preferred, persistent social tendencies are subjected to any form of social control . . . social remembering is very apt to take on a constructive and inventive character, either wittingly or unwittingly. Its manner then tends to become assertive, rather dogmatic and confident, and recall will probably be accompanied by excitement and emotion." [82]

In an experiment by Beier [83] it is found that anxiety can reduce abstract abilities generally and especially a loss of flexibility in intellectual functioning and visual coordination.

It is not only the stress arising out of the incident reported that affects testimony. Most witnesses, of course, are under tension caused by internal and external pressures of the courtroom

---

[80] See Hutchins & Slesinger, *op. cit. supra* note 9. Diminution of accuracy through rumor is like that of the curve of forgetting, with the number of details eliminated at once being greatest. A sharpening process occurs, in which unusual words or episodes are retained and may be elaborated upon; there is also a leveling, or condensing, taking place, and assimilation by the hearer of that which he hears of his own experience. The last is the major source of distortion. Leveling, sharpening, and assimilation occur simultaneously, and result in the "falsification . . . so characteristic of rumor." Allport & Postman, *The Basic Psychology of Rumor,* in READINGS IN SOCIAL PSYCHOLOGY 54, 65 (Maccoby, Newcomb & Hartley 3d ed. 1958).

[81] See Bartlett, *op. cit. supra* note 79, at 53.

[82] *Id.*

[83] *Effect of Induced Anxiety on Flexibility of Intellectual Functioning,* PSYCHOLOGICAL MONOGRAPHS 326 (1952).

situation. Lewis Carroll captured the feeling of a witness taking the stand by having the King of Hearts say to the witness: "Give your evidence, and don't be nervous, or I'll have you executed on the spot." [84] This is particularly understandable on cross-examination, which may well be described as a duel between a cross-examiner and a witness.

In stressful situations we are inclined to be influenced by the behavior of others who give us cues to propriety. "Particularly in ambiguous, unusual, or threatening situations, people are prone to judge the appropriateness of their behavior by looking to what others do. This phenomenon, termed by French and Raven 'referent power . . .,' has been demonstrated repeatedly in a variety of research contexts." [85] Even without stress, as reviewed by Collins and Raven,[86] pedestrians were found to be more likely to jaywalk, subjects more likely to volunteer for an experiment, and people more likely to violate a "no trespassing" sign when they found others doing so.

The kind of detail that a witness is asked to report generally falls into the category of "incidental memory." Hugo Münsterberg asked a class of 100 students to observe one hand while spinning a color wheel with the other and 18 students reported seeing only the spinning color wheel. Münsterberg also staged in his classroom the classic incident in which a prearranged but unannounced battle took place, culminating in the firing of a shot. The variations in the accounts of the incident written immediately afterward are great, but not random. Those most upset by the episode were least accurate in reporting it, those totally unaffected were somewhat more accurate, and those who were moderately involved emotionally were most accurate in reporting. These were untrained

---

[84] CARROLL, op. cit. supra note 34.

[85] Gathering Evidence: Problems and Pitfalls of Eyewitness Identification, Levine & Tapp, p. 18, citing French, J.R.P. & Raven, B.H. The Bases of Social Power, in (D. Cartwright ed.), STUDIES IN SOCIAL POWER, Ann Arbor, Mich., Univ. of Michigan Institute for Social Research (1959).

[86] Group Structure: Attraction, Coalitions, Communication, and Power, in THE HANDBOOKS OF SOCIAL PSYCHOLOGY Vol. 4 (2d ed. G. Lindzey & E. Aronson), Reading, Mass.: Addison-Wesley (1969).

and unprepared observers, presumably with no stake in either side of the sham conflict.[87] Even experienced observers whose attention has already been drawn to a shock-producing episode will differ in their observations. For example, Hutchins and Slesinger excerpt an editorial from *The New York World* that described the great disparities in eight newspaper reports of a simple situation in which Kerensky, on the speaker's platform, was slapped. The eight published reports all differed as to the sequence of events, Kerensky's reaction, and other integral aspects of a simple, brief, and unique episode.[88]

We can easily speculate on how much greater the variations would have been if the accounts had been written a year later, or after discussing the incident with others who had been present, or at the request of one of the parties to the conflict. Yet such accounts are usually the basis for determining liability — after an automobile accident for example — and criminal guilt.

We realize that a person's recall of a conversation reflects his interpretation of what took place, the selective process discussed above.[89] This interpretation-selection will be in terms of the person's expectations, but there is frequently difficulty in determining what his expectations are. What is his estimate of the probabilities of what was said? What is his estimate of the desirability of an outcome? It is such questions that determine the form taken by selective memory. "It is not always safe to rely upon a person's verbal report of his expectations because custom and convention make it difficult or embarrassing to express certain kinds of hopes and ambitions, particularly those which might conflict with the interests of other persons. . . ." [90]

A rule permitting *refreshment of recollection* is a further legal

---

[87] This experiment is reported in Hutchins & Slesinger, *Some Observations on the Law of Evidence,* 28 COLUM. L. REV. 432, 437 (1928). And see MÜNSTERBERG, ON THE WITNESS STAND: ESSAYS IN PSYCHOLOGY AND CRIME 15-36, 50 (1923) and PSYCHOLOGY: GENERAL AND APPLIED 396, ch. 30 (1915).

[88] Hutchins & Slesinger, *op. cit. supra* note 87, at 438.

[89] See pp 25-28 *supra.* Also, Touster, *Law and Psychology, How the Twain Might Meet,* 5 AMERICAN BEHAVIORAL SCIENTIST 3 (1962).

[90] See STOGDILL, *op. cit. supra* note 62, at 63-64.

recognition of the imperfections of memory. But allowance of such refreshment assumes that the recollection thus refreshed will be essentially accurate, that it is latent in the witness's mind and will be brought to the fore, intact, by his seeing or hearing an echo of the initial occurrence. The witness may be shown something he had written soon after the incident. Then he may "recall" either his original observation or, at least, having written it down at that time. Although this may meet the problem of the fallibility of memory, it leaves open the basic question whether the observation was accurate in the first instance.

The "refreshment of recollection" that the law permits deals with that "refreshment" conducted in the courtroom, before the judge and jury. But it cannot be doubted that the more common form of refreshment takes place before the trial, when the attorney prepares the case and interviews the witnesses. As the *Columbia Report* observed, "The distinction between coaching witnesses and preparing a case for trial is unfortunately too fine to be universally observed. Even deliberate perjury is resorted to; witnesses sometimes testify to the details of an accident they have never seen, or deliberately lie about the things they have seen." [91] The authors of that report, leading members of the bar, asserted that witnesses to motor vehicle accidents were especially susceptible to such pressures.[92]

The impact of *suggestion* on recollection cannot be exaggerated. It is known to the law and social science in numerous forms. "Refreshment" can be suggestion; it can also increase the distortion of memory. An instance noted by Hutchins and Slesinger [93] was an experiment in which all those present at an event were asked soon after to write a report of it. Some of them had also been allowed to read an inaccurate newspaper account of it. Those who read the newspaper account described the event as it was reported; those who did not read the story presented far more accurate accounts based on their own unrefreshed recollections. For a fuller discussion see Chapter V.

---

[91] COMM. TO STUDY COMPENSATION FOR AUTOMOBILE ACCIDENTS; REPORT TO THE COLUMBIA UNIVERSITY COUNCIL FOR RESEARCH IN THE SOCIAL SCIENCES 38 (1932).

[92] See also McCarty, note 16, *supra.* .

[93] Hutchins & Slesinger, *Some Observations on the Law of Evidence — Memory,* 41 HARV. L. REV. 860, 869 (1928).

Scientific reports have indicated that the witness's spontaneous narrative is more accurate (as well as more interesting and more impressive to a jury) than his testimony in response to step-by-step interrogation, although the latter may be more complete. The danger here is that the witness may acquiesce in a false suggestion. It is for this reason that in general "leading" questions may not be asked of one's own witness; but the definition of leading is far from precise.[94]

Though counsel may not lead his own witness and thus, in effect, testify through him, opposing counsel is free to suggest testimony under cross-examination by means of leading questions. Leading questions are permitted on cross-examination on the theory that broad scope must be given in order to test memory, veracity, and accuracy. It was undoubtedly an improvement to permit the impeachment of witnesses and no longer to accept as true their statements because they were under oath.[95] We have made progress by eliminating the mystical quality of early evidentiary proof, such as the oath, ordeal, and battle. Still, one might well subject to empirical research the question of the degree to which answers suggested by the cross-examiner distort the witness's report of what he observed and recalled, in addition to the research reported in Chapter IV.

We still require far more data than is available to understand the effects of *suggestion*.[96] However, we do have certain findings about interaction between and among people, which are relevant here. We know that some people are more susceptible to suggestion than others. For example, a person who is oriented to personalities — one who tends to get cues for his beliefs and actions from people with authority or status or others from whom he needs psychological support — is more likely to be susceptible to the cues given by others than "content-oriented" personalities, those who get their cues from the phenomena of the problems

[94] McCormick, Laws of Evidence (1954).

[95] See 2 Pollock & Maitland, The History of English Law 600 (2d ed. 1898).

[96] But see Asch, *The Effects of Group Pressures upon the Modification and Distortion of Judgments,* in Cartwright & Zander, *op. cit. supra* note 76, at 189; Siegel & Siegel, *Reference Groups, Membership Groups, and Attitude Change,* in Cartwright & Zander, *op. cit. supra* note 76, at 232; and Sherif, The Psychology of Social Norms 96-108 (1936).

which they face.[97] Consequently, a witness oriented to personalities will look to the judge for cues and when he gets none will look to the attorney who is examining or cross-examining him, to another witness, or even to a newspaper account of the case. The content-oriented witness will tend to seek his cues from events and objects, however imperfect his perceptions, rather than from persons; although it is improbable any normal person would be completely free from the effects of interaction with others.

From this we see that the "reality" brought to the case is a function not only of the perception of the witness but also of his individual personality and of situation, including the situation of the event testified to, the situation of the preparation of the case for trial, and the situation of the courtroom.

It is assumed that cross-examination will bring out truth and unveil false or inaccurate testimony. While it is true that a witness can be challenged on the accuracy of his observation, the point here made is not that the observation of the individual witness may be at fault but that on the whole the observation of all witnesses is faulty in some degree or in some situations. We bring to our observation of events preconceptions based upon experience. Our experience gives rise in us to expectations which color what we observe. And cognitive knowledge of the facts does not necessarily act to correct faulty observation.

For example, the author had read about the perceptual experiments used in the *Ames* demonstrations before he saw them (including the trapezoid mentioned on page 19, the distorted room, the lights of varying brightness, etc.).[98] Nevertheless, as had been the case with many other observers of the exhibition, his perceptions were as inaccurate as those of persons who had no knowledge of the exhibits before seeing them. Expectations on the cognitive level were not sufficient to overcome expectations on the

---

[97] See McDavid, Jr., *Personality and Situational Determinants of Conformity,* 58 J. ABNORMAL & SOCIAL PSYCHOLOGY 241, 246 (1959).

[98] These demonstrations devised by the late Adelbert Ames, Jr. and set up by Professor Hadley Cantril at Princeton in connection with his pioneer work in transactional psychology, and removed to Brooklyn College, include the trapezoid above mentioned, the distorted room, the lights of varying brightness, etc.

observational level. In the distorted room the face in the small window appeared larger than the face in the large window.

Reproduced from Explorations in Transactional Psychology, New York University Press (1961), by permission of the author, M. Lawrence, Studies in Human Behavior (1949), and the Publisher, Princeton University Press.

The brighter light looked closer than the dimmer light although in fact they were at the same distance. This does not mean that if faced with the need to act the author would not have resolved the incongruity existing between his observation and his cognition by choosing the latter as the determining factor in taking action. That assumes that he would have both time for recognition and for resolution of the incongruity. But if he had to act instantaneously, as the driver of a car or a pedestrian generally must, it would be the inaccurate observation which would control his behavior.

Psychological findings indicate that there is no evidence that a person will behave in the same way in all situations. Each situation, including interaction with other people, affects behavior; and different variables in each situation may cause different behavior by the same person. Thus, a man who will tell the truth and be shocked at the assertion that he could do anything but tell the truth under oath might well commit perjury in another circumstance. This should throw doubt upon the rule that "character for truth is always and everywhere admissible." Wigmore explains the relevance of the rule on the ground that the probability of telling the truth can be evaluated by the witness's "quality or tendency as to truth-telling in general, *i.e.,* his *veracity,* or, as more commonly and more loosely put, his *character for truth.*"[99] This would assume that "character" is consistent and independent of the pressures of the situation and the witness's interaction with others involved.

It is often assumed, too, that people always know when they are not telling the truth. False testimony can sometimes be based on false memories and perceptions which are frequently symptomatic of mental illness. For example, "The need to sacrifice another human being at the altar of one's guilt-laden conscience is one of the difficult sources of memory distortion which enter into all cases in which someone who has confessed guilt of past crimes turns and accuses others, whether of private offenses, criminal acts or acts of treason and subversion."[100]

False testimony may be intentional and conscious; on the other hand it may involve *psychological denial* by the witness that he is testifying falsely, that is, he may be blocking out the truth and not recognize he is doing so. Freud explained this process by his finding that "the ego often finds itself in the position of warding off some claim from the *external world* which it feels as painful, and that this is affected by *denying* the perceptions that bring to knowledge such a demand on the part of reality."[101] Doctor Lewin in discussing Freud's concept adds, "Denial disclaims the external world, then, as repression disclaims the instincts."[102]

---

[99] 3 WIGMORE, EVIDENCE § 922, at 447 (3d ed. 1940).

[100] Kubie, *Implications for Legal Procedure of the Fallibility of Human Memory,* 108 U. PA. L. REV. 59-75, at 70 (1959).

[101] FREUD, AN OUTLINE OF PSYCHOANALYSIS 118 (1949).

[102] LEWIN, THE PSYCHOANALYSIS OF ELATION 52-53 (1950).

Festinger suggests that where there is "a cluster of cognitive elements corresponding to some very important action a person has taken, an action to which he has committed himself in such a way that changing the action is almost impossible," something may occur that impinges on this person's cognition, creating a strong dissonance with the cognition. If he cannot successfully reduce such a conflict-dissonance by acquiring new evidence or arguments in support of the original cognition, he will probably attempt to deny the validity of the event which caused the dissonance.[103]

We see this when a witness who has told his story on direct examination is confronted with conflicting statements made by himself or other witnesses. In his desire not to look foolish the witness may change his testimony that now seems to him neither logical nor sensible. On the other hand, he may feel he has "committed himself in such a way that changing the action" is impossible. The more often he has had to repeat his testimony the more he will tend to believe it and find it impossible to change what he said. The contradictory statements with which he is confronted, which create a conflict with what he has testified, may cause him to deny the existence of the dissonant, the contradictory statements. *This denial* is not a simple verbalized denial — not just saying "No" — but an ego defense causing him to block out recognition that the contradictory statements are realities. Such behavior *should* properly discredit a witness — not as a perjurer, but because he is denying reality; however, presumably to the triers of fact, he will appear to be a perjurer, not a mere incredible witness.

The fusing and multiplying of experiences also occur and reduce the accuracy of recall.

"In one emotional state multiple experiences can be fused and then be represented in memory as though they had been one event. This happens constantly in childhood, as when a child may recall as a single startling event something that may have happened a hundred times. This is one form of what is called technically a 'screen memory.' Every adult does this too. On the other hand,

---

[103] FESTINGER, A THEORY OF COGNITIVE DISSONANCE 235-43 (1957).

that same child or adult may recall one single event as though it had happened many times. This is another potential source of guileless discrepancies in juridical testimony." [104]

Few witnesses testify without advance knowledge of what details would be most helpful to the party for whom they are testifying. The witness's recollection is affected by the fact that he has been asked to testify by a particular participant, and therefore the witness's interest becomes entwined with that of the party for whom he appears. (See Chapter III). These are "adversary" proceedings, and if *his* side wins the witness shares in a form of social reward that reinforces his "self-constancy." Unless he is merely answering a subpoena duces tecum, he can rarely avoid identifying with one side or the other, and the result will be either the endorsement of his commitment resulting from success of *his* party or frustration through failure of his side.[105]

With regard to criminal cases, reference has already been made to the suggestive effects of the police lineup in identification of suspects and will be further considered in Chapter II. In many instances the victim is especially susceptible to suggestions by the police or the district attorney because in his hostile state toward an offender he is eager to find a likely object for his hostility. A witness for the prosecution in a criminal case usually wants to be helpful. Sometimes there is a threat, or at least he feels a threat, if he does not cooperate with the prosecutor. Accomplices and co-conspirators are particularly susceptible to pressures by the prosecution. They have something to gain, they hope, by being cooperative.

The prosecutor may find conflicting pieces of evidence on specific detail, and he must put together a consistent story. The same is true of the attorney for the defense and attorneys in civil cases. If the attorney can bring the witnesses together, each witness tends to be influenced substantially by what the others have said in his presence, or if they are not present, by what the attorney represents that the other witnesses have said. By making

---

[104] Kubie, *op. cit. supra* note 100, at 68.

[105] Kilpatrick & Cantril, *The Constancies in Social Perception,* in EXPLORATIONS IN TRANSACTIONAL PSYCHOLOGY 354 (Kilpatrick ed. 1961).

the parts fit together there is a reduction of contradictory elements and thus of tension.[106]

Moreover, no witness wants to look foolish. He wants, whenever possible, not to be in conflict with other witnesses on his side. If others are saying something slightly different from what he has said, his confidence in his own perceptions tends to be weakened and his confidence that the views of others may be the correct ones increases. He is then likely to deny the evidence of his own senses and alter his beliefs to concur with those of others.[107] This same process — the weakening of confidence in one's own belief — also occurs, as we shall see, in the jury room.

When a witness identifies with one side of a case it is similar to becoming a member of a group. In effect his "group" is composed of a party and other witnesses on the side of the case for which he is testifying. It has been found that there is a tendency to assume beliefs of the members of the group which one joins. So, too, the witness gains reinforcement from supporting the beliefs of his side.[108]

William A. White said: "An unprejudiced individual does not exist." This, of course, was the theory of Khrushchev in proposing a troika in place of the Secretary General of the United Nations to replace Dag Hammarskjöld. Nevertheless, changing one's role may change one's prejudices [109] (or cause one to be more aware of and more on guard against them). Use of scientific method reduces prejudice to a minimum, because its essence is that all experiments must be subject to replication by others. So unless all the experimenters shared in the same prejudice a mistaken conclusion would not check out.

Just as observation may be influenced by what the observer feels would be to his advantage, so a witness who knows that it would

---

[106] Festinger & Aronson, *The Arousal and Reduction of Dissonance in Social Contexts,* in CARTWRIGHT & ZANDER, *op. cit. supra* note 76, at 214.

[107] Asch, *Effects of Group Pressures upon the Modification and Distortion of Judgments,* in CARTWRIGHT & ZANDER, *op. cit. supra* note 76, at 189.

[108] Siegel & Siegel, *Reference Groups, Membership Groups, and Attitude Change,* in CARTWRIGHT & ZANDER, *op. cit. supra* note 76, at 232.

[109] Lark, *How Foremen Get That Way,* DUNN'S REVIEW & MODERN INDUSTRY, Jan. 1955; FESTINGER, *op. cit. supra* note 103, at 274.

be advantageous if he were to remember that the light was red, or that the fire engine was sounding its siren, or the suspect had declared his intention to avenge himself on the victim, may ultimately believe that this was what he saw or heard. Thus a woman sitting with her rear over the window ledge cleaning her third-story window while elevated trains were passing testified she heard the defendant on the street threaten to kill the victim just before the shot was fired. She volunteered her testimony to the district attorney and was a neighborhood heroine. She came to this observation when she read that the defendant and the defendant's former paramour had been talking together on the corner just before the defendant fired the shots. What would have been more natural, then, than that she had threatened to kill him? (P.S. The lady was acquitted.) Interestingly, in the same case a woman detective testified falsely to a conversation several days before the killing in which she claimed the defendant threatened to commit murder. When asked to produce her police report and the police blotter she presented a false report which she had typed during the course of her testimony. If either story had been believed the lady might have burned.[110] If a witness's actual recollection is vague or nonexistent then any dissonance or contradiction can be removed or any void filled by slight but welcome advantage to himself, especially some psychological ego advantage.[111]

C. ARTICULATION

The final stage at which the witness's account may be distorted is in its *articulation.* After he has seen, interpreted, and recalled the incident, he must convert his mental image into words that will communicate this image to his hearers. This translation of images into words leads to two kinds of distortion: the use of words creates a compulsion to fill in the gaps in a narrative, and gives no indication to the hearer of how clear to the witness is the image that he is reporting. Words fail to describe accurately the perception they report, or whether it is in effect an inference and not a percept. For instance, if the witness says, "It was raining and

---

[110] See LEVY, MY DOUBLE LIFE 159-62 (1958).

[111] Cohen, *Attitudinal Consequences of Induced Discrepancies Between Cognition and Behavior,* 24 PUBLIC OPINION Q. 297 (1960).

I wore my rubbers," we cannot know whether he recalls one of those facts and infers the other, recalls both, or has deduced both from a third recollection, *e.g.,* that he saw people carrying umbrellas.[112]

Language itself, Kilpatrick and Cantril believe, serves as a rigidifying process, creating "slippage between the abstraction as it *functions* in behavior and abstraction as it is *named.* There is a basic tendency to treat whatever is perceived as both concrete and absolute, despite its abstract and nonabsolute nature. To do otherwise is to inhibit the rapid and effective action necessary to the process of living." [113] Words are, of course, symbolic of objective realities and ideals. They are a shorthand, an essential but incomplete method of communicating individual experience. As symbols, they connote different experiences to different persons. It is not possible to reproduce in words the overtones and prismatic colors, and particularly the feeling, of the situation described. Court and jury get at best a reproduction of an abstract. "We tear ourselves to pieces because of symbols, and we are more vulnerable to this than to any host of predators." [114]

One is reminded of the various uses of language by Irwin Edman: "Language is a scandalously ambiguous instrument. It is a way of describing objective and verifiable things, in the context of practical control, or it is a lyric cry, an automatic soliloquy. It is sometimes statistics and sometimes song." [115] And, we might add, sometimes a screen to true thought and feeling.

Accent and pronunciation may also result in misperceptions. At a meeting one time, a speaker was referring to a "ten-year plan," but to the author it sounded like "tenure plan," and it was only after several repetitions that the author fitted this phrase into context (the expectation of appropriateness) and understood it as it was intended, not as it was pronounced.

D. SOME RULES OF EVIDENCE

Other rules of evidence which deserve consideration relate to declarations against interest, self-serving declarations, and

---

[112] Hutchins & Slesinger, *op. cit. supra* note 93, at 860, 867.

[113] Kilpatrick & Cantril, *op. cit. supra* note 105, at 361.

[114] THOMAS, THE LIVES OF A CELL (1974).

[115] EDMAN, FOUR WAYS OF PHILOSOPHY 208-09 (1937).

testifying to conclusions. In a psychological sense a *declaration against interest* (which is admissible in evidence) is just as much a self-serving declaration as any other declaration (which the law excludes from evidence), for it is motivated by, and is an expression of, a need. Because the law searches for guilt or liability rather than reality or truth as a basis for judgment, it welcomes confessional evidence and rejects as unreliable attempts at justification through explanations that are self-defensive. Neither declarations against interest nor self-serving declarations may be in themselves true, but either may reveal truth. The circumstances in which they are made and the turn of their phrasing may illuminate more than their intended meaning. Good cross-examiners have long been aware of this and since the teachings of Freud have become common knowledge people have been increasingly alert to such cues to meaning in daily life. But the rules of the game of litigation are founded on the belief that self-serving declarations will be taken literally and must be excluded.

Similarly, a witness is not trusted to *volunteer* the reasons he comes to a *conclusion, i.e.,* his inferences. Instead he is directed to testify to what he saw or heard and he thus frequently testifies to his conclusion as being his observation. Of course, as we have noted, much of observation is a conclusion, a filling in of gaps in perception by experience and expectation. Surely a more accurate evaluation of perception would be possible if the process of filling in gaps and arriving at conclusions were laid on the table. Again, to the psychiatrist and psychologist this process would be just as revealing of reality as any statement of perception and helpful in evaluating the accuracy of a perception.

This detailed account of what we know about how the individual perceives and acts in relation to the world around him indicates some basic flaws in the presumptions which the rules of evidence apply to accounts by witnesses. The disparity between man as a legal concept and as a knowledgeable organism from a scientific view is so great that it serves to make our law seem inappropriate and therefore unworthy of the respect in which we desire it held. Scholars in the area of evidence have been aware of some of the disparities between legal hypotheses and scientific data. McCormick notes, for instance, that the distribution in admissibility between fact and opinion is "clumsy because its basic assumption is an illusion. . . . There is no conceivable statement that is not in some measure the product of inference and reflection as well as observation and memory." [116] He praises courts' increasing flexibility on this matter, although the distinction drawn in this country between inference and memory is more rigid than in England, where it originated.

Courts also have been commended for acknowledging to some extent the scientific findings about recollection and refreshment. The former rule had been that if a witness's prior statement were introduced as conflicting with his testimony on the stand it could be considered only in terms of impeaching the witness's credibility. But courts have been increasingly permissive about the use of the prior statement substantively, since it should in fact have more merit than the testimony on the stand because it would have been made earlier. [117]

But this progress in a few limited areas makes more acute the need for a complete reconsideration of the rules of evidence to conform them overall instead of piecemeal to what we know of the human condition. Only in that way can the law maintain its mediating role in our society. In fact, this liberalization of certain rules still remains within the framework of litigation as an adversary proceeding, rather than as a search for truth.

---

[116] McCORMICK, *op. cit. supra* note 94.

[117] See Hand, J., in *DiCarlo v. United States,* 6 F.2d 364 (1925) and in *United States v. Block et al.,* 88 F.2d 618 (1937); also Swan, in *United States v. Corsi,* 65 F.2d 564 (1933); and 3 WIGMORE, EVIDENCE § 1018(b), at 687 (3d ed. 1940).

CHAPTER II

IDENTIFICATION

"I'll Never Forget That Face."

Identification is a critical phase of perception and recall. Life, liberty, repute and recompense as well as discovery of violations of civil and criminal law often depend on proper identification. Nevertheless, perception is often at its least reliable in identification. All the limitations of perception under stress apply. So does suggestibility. Tensions at the time of a happening may be great. The opportunity for precise vision or sharp hearing may be absent. Frequently people have difficulty distinguishing features of persons of another race. This is particularly true of identification of blacks by whites, especially in poor light.[118]

Williams discusses identification evidence from the experience of the British courts and cites a number of British experiments that are in agreement with those in this country. He also quotes a study by Grophe in which the latter says "Resemblance is a matter of relativity. For a white person, all negroes are like each other, and conversely. A person can much better distinguish those of his own age and condition than those of different ages and conditions. Uniform is a cause of fallacious resemblance, above all for those who do not wear it."[119]

"I'll never forget that face as long as I live" is a statement of certainty many times proven to be in error. No year passes in which the press does not tell us of cases of false identity, often of persons who have served years in prison because of a complainant who would "never forget."

---

[118] Seeleman, *The Influence of Attitude upon the Remembering of Pictorial Material*, ARCHIVES OF PSYCHOLOGY, No. 258, (1940); Malpass & Kravitz, *Recognition for Faces of Own and Other Race*, J. PERSONALITY & SOCIAL PSYCHOLOGY, 13, 330-34 (1969).

[119] WILLIAMS, THE PROOF OF GUILT (1963); ch. V, Mistaken Evidence Identification, 106-24; and citing GROPHE, LA CRITIQUE DU TEMOIGNAGE 212-18 (1927).

New Yorker, January 8, 1979 at 27. Reprinted with permission.

In a case recently reported in the newspaper, a cab driver was arrested when he was identified by a building superintendent as the man who had held him up and robbed him. On conviction he could have received a 15 year sentence. He was released when he was able to show that, at the time of the robbery, he was arguing about a parking ticket at a Parking Violations Bureau. Most accused persons in a situation similar to that of this cabby would be unable to obtain credible witnesses to an alibi.

In 1970 there was a holdup in a bar by a gunman who shot and killed the bartender. One, Jackson, was in a police station on an unconnected matter and there was allegedly recognized by a witness to the murder. The three other witnesses were called and after seeing a lineup of six men including Jackson, all four witnesses identified him. Three of the witnesses had seen him sitting alone shortly before the lineup. All four of them identified Jackson at the trial. There was no other evidence connecting him in any way with the crime.

Prior to Jackson's identification four witnesses had looked at numerous "mug shots" and said one them resembled the gunman. The man had also been named by an informer. Following the identification of Jackson, however, this lead was dropped by the police.

After serving eight years in prison the Circuit Court of Appeals (Second Circuit) affirming a decision by the District Court, freed Jackson. Judge Lumbard, in writing for the court, noted "the dangers of convicting on identification testimony alone are well known to those whose duty it is to prosecute crime." In Jackson's case the court said that "the police were content to consider the case solved in reliance on questionable identification procedures and despite the fact that positive identification regarding other suspects had been called to their attention."

Despite the terrible misfortune of having to spend eight years in prison, how fortunate Jackson was that there was no mandatory death penalty in the State of New York.*

"Errors of recognition can no longer be counted; a volume would not suffice to contain all those that have been discovered, and that is only a small part of the whole. They pertain above all to the

---

* N.Y. Times, Dec. 23, 1978, at A1.

identification of persons." [120] This unreliability, together with the risks of suggestion, are relevant to confrontations whether they are called lineups, identification parades, showups or presentations of a suspect alone to a witness. In every form there are "dangers inhering in eyewitness identification," as Mr. Justice Brennan said in *U.S. v. Wade*.[121] Moreover, he said, once a witness has selected the accused "he is not likely to go back on his word later on, so that in practice the issue of identity may (in the absence of other relevant evidence) for all practical purposes be determined there and then, before the trial." [122] Just as an accused may come to believe in his or her erroneous confession, so too a witness may become convinced of an erroneous perception as a result of even subtle pressures or self-persuasion.[123]

Wall [124] relates various techniques used by the police in lineups and other confrontations to cause the identifying witness to believe that only one person can be the suspect. For example, four policemen (presumably out of uniform), two at each end, look at the fifth man in the middle. The suspect is declared to be small, so there is only one small man in the lineup. He has been described as shabby, so there is only one shabby person in the lineup, etc. The tricks of the police trade are documented (with recommendations) by Inbau and Reid.[125]

Participants in a lineup with the accused are frequently police officers and the identity of the participants is rarely recorded or divulged at a trial. Because of the disadvantage an unsupported defendant has in trying to prove improper identification procedures outside the courtroom, the Court held in *Wade* that the defendant is entitled to be represented by attorney at such a proceeding.

We are all sensitive to what those with whom we are interacting

---

[120] GROPHE, *op. cit.* 309 and 283 concerning mistakes in the recall of colors, quoted in WILLIAMS, *op. cit.*

[121] 388 U.S. 218, 229, 87 S.Ct. 1926, 1933 (1967).

[122] *Id.*

[123] Bem, *Inducing Belief in False Confessions,* 3 J. PERSONALITY AND SOCIAL PSYCHOLOGY 707 (1966); Bem, *When Saying Is Believing,* PSYCHOLOGY TODAY, 21 (June 1967); Insko, *Verbal Reinforcement of Attitude,* 2 J. PERSONALITY AND SOCIAL PSYCHOLOGY 621 (1965).

[124] EYEWITNESS IDENTIFICATION IN CRIMINAL CASES (1965). And for a splendid discussion of criminal identification see COHN & UDOLF, THE CRIMINAL JUSTICE SYSTEM AND ITS PSYCHOLOGY (1979).

[125] CRIMINAL INTERROGATION AND CONFESSIONS (1967).

think and feel. Others are able to influence our expectations and, consequently, our perception and recall. To retain self-image we tend to conform.[126] In other words, we are suggestible in varying degrees by various persons in different situations. Identifying witnesses are no exceptions. Moreover, almost all of us, four fifths says Dr. Herbert Spiegel,[127] are to one degree or another subject to hypnotic effects. This does not mean that we must be put into a trance by a hypnotist. Many people have hypnotic powers unknown to themselves or others. Many, unknown to themselves and others, are readily influenced by such people. Dr. Spiegel, a psychiatrist, who has done research in hypnosis and law, concluded: "Under the duress of interrogation in the police station or on the witness stand, the accused or the witness can unwittingly shift into the hypnotic mode, thus giving the interrogator the power of a hypnotist whether he knows it or not."

Whether or not a witness may "shift into the hypnotic mode" an identifying witness may be under stress arising from the event, whether criminal or civil, in which he or she was a victim or participant, or because of the circumstances in which identification is sought. The witness may be subject to fatigue from many causes including possible prolonged periods of waiting, extended interrogation, anxiety as to possible claims of personal involvement, worry that there will be further interrogations and possible appearances on a witness stand. Any of these may cause the cues of others to be attractive.

If someone is apprehended at the scene of a crime and is immediately identified by a witness, or a showup takes place within a few minutes after the crime is committed,[128] the psychological problems of lineup identifications are not apt to be present.

---

[126] SHERIF, PSYCHOLOGY OF SOCIAL NORMS (1936), see *post.* p. 131.

[127] *Hypnosis and Invasion of Privacy,* in HOW TO DEFEND A CRIMINAL CASE, 355 (Lawyer & George eds. 1967). See also Foster, *Confessions and the Station House Syndrome,* DE PAUL L. REV. XVIII (1969) and Driver, *Confessions and the Social Psychology of Coercion,* HARV. L. REV. 82, 1, 42-61 (1968).

[128] See *McRae v. U.S.,* 137 U.S. App. D.C. 80, 87, 420 F.2d 1283, 1290 (1969). In a footnote in *Manson v. Brathwaite,* 432 U.S. 98, 131, 97 S.Ct. 2243, 2261 (1977), Mr. Justice Marshall points out: ". . . Reviewing a number of its cases, the Court of Appeals for the District of Columbia Circuit concluded several years ago that while showups occurring up to perhaps 30 minutes after a crime are generally permissible, one taking place four hours later, far removed from the crime scene, was not." Citing *McRae v. United States, supra.*

However, there are intermediate cases such as that in *Kirby v. Illinois*.[129] In that case two men were stopped for interrogation. Each produced as identification items that bore the name of Shard. After their arrest and after they had been taken to the police station, the officers learned that there had been a robbery of one Shard two days before. Shard was brought to the station house and identified the two men as the robbers. The Court held that, although this showup took place after the arrest, there had been no indictment or other form of charge for criminal offense. Consequently, there was no criminal prosecution that entitled the prisoner to representation by counsel.

The dissenting opinion in *Kirby* found no reason "for concluding that a post-arrest confrontation for identification, unlike a post-charge confrontation, is not among those 'critical confrontations of the accused by the prosecution at pretrial proceedings where the results might well settle the accused's fate and reduce the trial itself to a mere formality.' " [130] The dissent goes on to say:

> "The highly suggestive form of confrontation employed in this case underscores the point. This showup was particularly fraught with the peril of mistaken identification. In the setting of a police station squad room where all present except petitioner and Bean [a co-defendant] were police officers, the danger was quite real that Shard's understandable resentment might lead him too readily to agree with the police that the pair under arrest, and the only persons exhibited to him, were indeed the robbers." [131]

In view of the station house syndrome, it is difficult to distinguish between pre-charge and post-charge confrontations. The same disadvantages are experienced in both situations by the suspect. He is alone. He is unable to reconstruct at his trial the events or atmosphere of the identification. And the dangers of suggestion (and possible hypnotic state) created by the station house, with only police present, contain the dangers on which the

---

[129] 406 U.S. 682, 92 S.Ct. 1877 (1972).
[130] *Op. cit.* U.S. 699, S.Ct. 1887.
[131] *Op. cit.* U.S. 699 and 700, S.Ct. 1887; see also Wall, *supra.*

Supreme Court based its opinion in *Wade.* The distinction between pre-charge and post-charge identification is logically and scientifically untenable.

Of course, as Levine and Tapp [132] point out: "Even if lawyers are permitted a more active role they may not be sufficiently sensitive to important psychological variables. In other words ... lawyers presence, whether active or passive, may have little or no effect on the dangers which the Court found [in *Wade*] inherent in pretrial confrontations upon which its holdings were in large part based."

The showup can be even more suspect than a lineup as a method of criminal identification. "In fact, the lineup procedure itself was developed by the British police because the showup, or formal one-to-one confrontation between witness and suspect, was considered so grossly suggestive and unfair." [133]

The police may be no more reliable as witnesses than other people. Levine and Tapp [134] refer to a report by the lawyer-novelist Erle Stanley Gardner in *The Court of Last Resort* (1952) in which he told of an empirical test indicating the inability of "trained, experienced" state police officers to estimate accurately height, weight and age. The respective variations were 5 inches, 20 pounds and 15 years.

Tables G and H in Chapter III show that in the experiment there described among the items reported by several categories of the witnesses, descriptions of the suspect person and clothing were more erroneous than items concerning action, background and sound. Table I indicates that the police trainees more than the other witnesses "perceived what had never happened."

In another study Toch writes:

"The fact that police work entails disproportionately many contacts with socially underprivileged and emotionally disturbed persons who do not display typical middle-class conduct, can shape police perception of human nature and of

---

[132] Levine & Tapp, *The Psychology of Criminal Investigation: The Gap From Wade to Kirby,* 121 U. PA. L. REV. 5, 1079, 1125 (1973).

[133] Levine & Tapp, *Gathering Evidence: Problems and Pitfalls of Eyewitness Identification,* in SOCIAL-PSYCHOLOGICAL ANALYSIS OF LEGAL PROCESSES (Ebbesen & Konecni eds.) in press, referring to Wall; *op. cit.* and Quinn, *In the Wake of Wade: The Dimensions of Eyewitness Identification Cases,* 42 U. COLO. L. REV., 135-58 (1970).

[134] Levine & Tapp, *op. cit.*

appropriate social behavior.... By thus unfavorably categorizing one segment of the community, the police create a double standard in human relations. Placement in the outgroup deprives a person of his right to customary courtesies, to friendly consideration and to frank communication." [135]

These experiences and the attitudes flowing from them create expectations on the part of the police and, consequently, affect their perception. This does not mean, of course, that in all situations and with respect to all persons of a lower socio-economic class the perception of the police is distorted. It should, however, be a signal to evaluate police testimony with special care when such persons are involved. Furthermore, by reason of these values the police may unwittingly cue witnesses called to identify suspects of lower socio-economic or racial groups. It is simple for an interrogator to give positive reenforcement to a witness by encouraging the witness to recall events as the interrogator prefers them. (See discussion in Chapter IV.)

What are the testimonial phenomena that make identification suspect? [136] Memory and perception are selective. Although as will be shown in Chapter IV memory can be stimulated by interrogation, it is not possible to perceive or recall most of the stimuli that reach one's senses of perception in a minute or two. Only those that for one cause or another have salience to the observer are readily retrievable.

A complainant or witness tends to want to answer questions. To say "I don't know" or "I don't remember" tends to make one feel foolish, and to appear to others to be stupid, unobservant. How can one confess to having no recollection of what the other driver did just before the impact or what the assaulting party looked like? Those called as witnesses to make identification in a lineup "quite

---

[135] Toch, *Psychological Consequences of the Police Role*, presented at a symposium at Annual Meeting of American Psychological Association, September 1, 1963. A study by Rokeach, Miller & Snyder found considerable differences in values between police and the policed: *The Value Gap Between Police and Policed*, JOURNAL OF SOCIAL ISSUES, 27 (2), 155-71 (1971).

[136] See generally Buckhout, *Eyewitness Testimony*, SCIENTIFIC AMERICAN 231 (6) 28 (1974) and Levine & Tapp, *op. cit. supra* note 132.

probably are concerned about performing well, being helpful, and not looking foolish.[137]

Often a witness may wish to gain self esteem or the esteem of others by being helpful. So he or she fills in the gaps in recall. In an anxiety arousing situation, under stress, the need to identify a wrong-doer may increase, although accuracy may be decreased. So there may occur a process of self-persuasion even leading to a belief in one's own confession. The original erroneous statement to an investigator or at a lineup will be fortified by repetition to an attorney in the case (especially in the presence of other witnesses agreeing among themselves).

In *Manson v. Brathwaite*[138] a police officer identified the accused from a single picture left on his desk by another police officer. The facts of the case are less important than the opinions, Mr. Justice Blackmun writing for the Court and Mr. Justice Marshall writing the dissent. Each might be considered an excellent law review article or, perhaps, briefs for the opposing parties on the subject of identification from photographs.

The discussion centered on whether there should be a *per se* or a "totality of the circumstances" approach to out-of-court identification evidence.[139] The *per se* "focuses on the procedures employed and requires the exclusion of the out-of-court identification evidence, without regard to reliability, whenever it has been obtained through unnecessarily suggestive confrontation procedures." On this approach the dissent was based. The totality of circumstances approach "permits the admission of the confrontation evidence if, despite the suggestive aspect, the out-of-court identification possesses certain features of reliability." The majority opinion accepted this view.

The majority argument is in reality a plea for a "practical" way, although the court in effect admits it is not the better way of treating identification. Mr. Justice Blackmun wrote:

"Of course, it would have been better had D'Onofrio presented Glover with a photographic array including 'so far as practicable . . . a reasonable number of persons similar to

---

[137] Levine & Tapp, *op. cit. supra* note 132.

[138] 432 U.S. 98, 97 S.Ct. 2243 (1977).

[139] *Op. cit.* U.S. 110, S.Ct. 2251.

any person then suspected whose likeness is included in the array.' Model Code ... § 160.2(2). The use of that procedure would have enhanced the force of the identification at trial and would have avoided the risk that the evidence would be excluded as unreliable. But we are not disposed to view D'Onofrio's failure as one of constitutional dimension to be enforced by a rigorous and unbending exclusionary rule. *The defect, if there be one, goes to weight and not to substance.*"[140] (Italics added.)

The Court, however, ignores the weight given to evidence offered by police officers concerning identification. It would be difficult for a jury to distinguish in these circumstances the weight from the substance. What witnesses to the transaction other than the officers could the accused call? How could the accused demonstrate at the trial any suggestion involved?

In the dissenting opinion Mr. Justice Marshall wrote:

"... The crux of the *Wade* decisions, however, was the unusual threat to the truth-seeking process posed by the frequent untrustworthiness of eyewitness identification testimony. This, combined with the fact that juries unfortunately are often unduly receptive to such evidence, is the fundamental fact of judicial experience ignored by the Court today."[141]

Citing *Simmons v. U.S.*[142] he also points out that the Court recognized the danger involved in photographic identification, and that a witness who had seen a suggestively displayed picture would "retain in his memory the image of the photograph rather than of the person actually seen ...."

Finally, as the dissenting opinion points out, the majority by dismissing "the corrupting effect of the suggestive identification" procedure in effect grants to the police "license to convict the innocent."[143] For the totality of circumstances principle is too

---

[140] *Op. cit.* U.S. 117, S.Ct. 2254.
[141] *Op. cit.* U.S. 119-20, S.Ct. 2255.
[142] 390 U.S. 377, 383-84, 88 S.Ct. 967 (1968).
[143] *Op. cit.* U.S. 98, S.Ct. 2262.

amorphous, too indifferent to the psychological impact of suggestion to ensure a fair trial.[144]

An experiment by Buckhout [145] is illustrative of the unreliability of identification testimony based on photographs. He and his associates staged an "attack" on a professor by a student before 141 witnesses. A bystander, another outsider, of the same age as the "attacker" was at the scene. After the incident the experimenters took sworn statements of the witnesses, asking each to describe the suspect and whatever he or she could recall about the happening. The passage of the time of the happening was overestimated by the witnesses by a factor of 2-1/2 to 1. The estimates of the "attacker's" weight averaged 14 percent too high. Age was slightly underestimated by 2 years. Including such items as appearance and dress, the accuracy score was 25 percent of the maximum possible score.

After 7 weeks the experimenters showed each witness a set of 6 photographs under 4 experimental conditions. They were given instructions of two kinds: (a) "low-bias," in which witnesses were asked only if they recognized anybody in the photographs and (b) "high-bias," in which witnesses were reminded of the attack incident, told that the researchers had an idea who the suspect was and asked the witnesses to find the attacker in one of two arrangements of photographs, all well-lit views of young men including the attacker and the bystander.

In the unbiased array, the 6 portraits were set out with facial expressions of a similar kind and similar clothing. However, in the biased spread the attacker had a "distinctive expression" and his portrait was positioned at an angle.

The suspect was correctly identified by only 40 percent of the witnesses. Twenty-five percent identified the innocent bystander. Even the professor who was attacked picked the innocent bystander. The "highest proportion of correct identifications, 61 percent, was achieved with a combination of a biased set of photographs and biased instructions." In that condition the degree of confidence expressed by the witnesses was significantly higher.

---

[144] For a summary of cases dealing with the identification process and especially photographic identification, see American Law Institute *Model Code of Pre-Arraignment Procedure,* § 160.2.

[145] *Op. cit. supra* note 136.

As noted earlier (and see Chapter IV), it was the better witnesses who tended to express less confidence than those who had impeached themselves.

Another experiment by Buckhout was conducted in conjunction with a news TV program. A film of a mugging was shown. Following it there was a picture of a 6-person lineup. Of the 2,145 viewers who called following the program, only 14.1 percent made an accurate identification of the mugger. This is only as many as one might expect by chance.[146]

This is one of a number of experiments by various people indicating the uncertainty of correct identification by photograph.

In addition to misperceptions and uncertainties of recall, there are psychological impairments of the identification process. People, for example, have a need to see in terms of their expectations which in turn may be cued by their biases and stereotypes. In a classic experiment, Allport and Postman showed to subjects a picture of a white man and a black man apparently arguing in a subway train. The white man held a razor. Over half of the subjects said that the razor was held by the black man and often that he was brandishing it in a threatening manner.[147]

False perceptions may consciously or unconsciously be induced by the police or other authority, because there is the tendency to respond to suggestibility, especially to the cues given by someone deemed to have authority.[148]

It is safer to please authority — a police officer or a prosecuting attorney — by following his cues, which may not be intentional, but are often purposeful, than to reject them. It is understandable for a witness to believe: after all, the police must have good reason for suspecting someone in a lineup, and surely in a showup. So Levine and Tapp (citing a number of research experiments) conclude: "Recognized or official power provides another substantial source of influence over individuals." [149]

This is in effect summarized in *Wade*: "We do not assume that these risks [those inherent in suggestive identification processes

---

[146] Buckhout, *op. cit. supra* note 136.

[147] THE PSYCHOLOGY OF RUMOR (1947).

[148] See Milgram experiment, ch. V *Post.*; and *Wade, op. cit.* U.S. 235, S.Ct. 1936.

[149] *Op. cit. Gathering Evidence: Problems and Pitfalls of Eyewitness Identification*, SOCIAL-PSYCHOLOGICAL ANALYSIS OF LEGAL PROCESSES (Ebbesen & Konecni eds.) (in press) *supra* note 133.

in the lineup] are the result of police procedures intentionally designed to prejudice an accused. Rather we assume they derive from the dangers inherent in eyewitness identification and the suggestibility inherent in the context of the pretrial identification." [150]

On the other hand, the victim or a witness may wish to avoid further connection with the happening and evade identification of an offender. This may be "perceptual defense" or psychological denial of recognition. He or she may want to escape from the episode by absorbing or recalling as little as possible of what occurred. Frequently, too, by evading identification a witness avoids the nuisance or embarrassment of the witness stand. Failure to identify, like misidentification, leaves the felon at large.

Wall [151] has suggested that lineups be conducted by police officers who are not connected with the investigation of crime. In this way police pressure and suggestion would significantly be reduced. This procedure has been followed in England, Paris and the District of Columbia. Of course, such a procedure would be more practicable in a city with a large police force than in a small community.

Levine and Tapp [152] suggest a number of regulations which could establish uniform procedures for identification, some of them already adopted. Nevertheless, although we know pretty well some of the psychological dangers implicit in identification procedures, further research on some of the proposals of improve identification is indicated. Some of these areas for research are well identified by Levine and Tapp.[153]

In summary, it can be said that identification of offenders, of

---

[150] *Wade, op. cit.* U.S. 235, S.Ct. 1936.

[151] *Op. cit.*

[152] *The Psychology of Criminal Identification: The Gap from Wade to Kirby, op. cit.* 1121 (1973). They suggest that the police be prohibited from having suspects dress in clothes, make gestures or utter words described by witnesses, if other participants in the lineup are not required to do the same; lineup victims should be of the same race and sex and approximately the same physically. They cite Wigmore's suggestion that there be prepared various photographs of different people in a number of stock movements, that the suspect be filmed in a similar manner, that some 25 such films be shown in succession to each witness who is to press a button indicating identification and the degree of hesitancy.

[153] *Op. cit.* 1122.

those who have broken criminal or tort laws, presents a critical phase of the unreliability of perception and recall. The court decisions concerning the validity of identifications, as represented by those of the Supreme Court, rely principally on inference and logic. Granted the empirical study of the pitfalls of identification is as yet inadequate. Nevertheless, courts have given little attention to what empirical research has demonstrated.

CHAPTER III

SOME VAGARIES OF RECALL*

Generally, in the trial of a case there is testimony which concerns a specific happening, that is, certain events which occurred between or among specific individuals at a particular time and place. In tort and criminal cases, witnesses are usually unprepared to see and hear what happens. The situation may be new to them. It usually is. Thus what they perceive and recall and what they may select to perceive and recall among the numerous items in any situation are functions not only of the situation but also of physiological and psychological fields determined by their individual experiences and physical condition.[154] The application to law of some of the empirical evidence already discovered has been reported in Chapter I.

There is a rich if incomplete literature on perception and recall. With few exceptions, however, the experiments reported have involved college students in more or less abstract situations. What has been said of Small Group research is also applicable to research of perception and recall.

"For one, much work is based on very restricted samples, namely, college students. In addition, some research is fairly basic in nature with little interest or attempt by scientists to apply their findings or to initiate studies to solve "real world" problems." [155]

This research has rarely involved the kind of situation applicable to litigation. Nowhere are perception and recall more intimately related to truth than in the trial of a case.

---

* This chapter is largely based on research done jointly by the author and Helge Mansson, Ph. D. in Social Psychology, with the assistance of John VanEsen.
[154] Kilpatrick & Cantril, *The Constancies in Social Perception, op. cit. supra* note 105.
[155] Altman (Naval Medical Research Institute), *Mainstream of Research on Small Groups*, 23, No. 4 PUB. ADMIN. REV. (1963).

If law is to be a successful instrument of state policy it is important that its efficacy be demonstrated. It is important, too, that there is some approximation of law, as it is applied by the courts, to legal theory (its premises) and to moral justifications. The findings of the social psychologists, as noted in the previous chapter, have indicated serious discrepancies. But since the pioneer work of Münsterberg [156] little has been done to attach the applicability of those findings to a situation at least approximating such as may arise in a court. One such situation, experimentally oriented, dealing with recall, is the subject of the following research.

Research by the author and his associates [157] attempted to study on a quantitative basis some of the factors involved in the process of recall by witnesses. No attempt was made to exhaust all possible factors influencing a person's selective recall. This chapter presents some of the results of their experiment in which they tried to examine how individuals of different educational and economic backgrounds perceive or recall a situation which might occur in the life of any of us and be the subject at issue in a trial as well as their misperceptions and inferences. We also attempted to demonstrate the effects of time delays in reporting on what had been perceived upon selective recall. Other variables will be discussed later.

A moving picture with sound, lasting 42 seconds, was shown to 167 law school students in the first month of their legal training, to 102 police trainees in the first month of their training in the Police Academy and to 22 people who attended a settlement house and who lived in low income housing, and most of whom were on relief, a total of 291 subjects.

Socio-Educational Status of Population Groups

The law students had all completed college and, with few exceptions, were all of a higher economic level than the police trainees, very few of whom had had any college education, but who had all completed high school. The police trainees, in turn, were of

---

[156] MÜNSTERBERG, *op. cit. supra* note 87.
[157] See footnote at beginning of ch. III.

a higher economic level than the settlement house people, only a few of whom had finished high school, and about half of whom had not reached high school.

Summary of Picture

The picture which we showed had background music through most of the sequence. It opened with a boy lowering a mosquito net on a baby carriage. The boy was in his late teens or early twenties, of average build, wore a dark jacket, lighter baggy slacks, and a white shirt open at the neck. There were white buttons on the jacket and around his neck there were two strings or chains with a flute or whistle on one and a looking glass on the other. He had sideburns, curly hair. The baby was crying. At the beginning, the boy was smiling at the baby carriage. He appeared uncertain or nervous. He faced the baby carriage and touched the handle and started rocking it, then he removed his hands from the handle. The baby cried louder. The boy rocked the baby carriage back and forth, shifting his weight from foot to foot. The rocking became more violent and he pulled the carriage backward off the grass on which it had been to the driveway. A woman called out or shouted, "Mrs. Gerard, Mrs. Gerard, quick! Someone's running away with your baby." The boy turned toward the fence of the yard and then toward the house. A woman came running from the house toward the boy and the carriage. The woman was young. She wore a white smock and a darker skirt. She shouted, "You bad boy! You bad boy!", and waved her left arm as she ran. The boy hesitated, looked startled, ran through the gate and crouched in a corner by a white picket fence near a bush growing through the fence. A mailbox was above his head. At this point the picture stopped.

At the opening the carriage was on the grass in front of the house. The carriage hood was up. It was a four-wheel carriage of a dark color with a patterned design; the mosquito netting covered the hood and open part of the carriage. There was a hem on the mosquito netting. There was a light colored cover in the carriage.

The yard itself had a white picket fence at the left and in front there was a gate and driveway which led to the house. There were three pieces of wicker furniture with cushions in the center of the lawn, two chairs and a settee. There was a tree in the yard and another white picket fence on the side with a shrub or rose bush. It was a time of the year when leaves were on the trees and shrubs.

The subjects of the experiment were asked to consider that they were walking around a corner and what they saw and heard was what they saw and heard in the picture. They were then asked to record what they had perceived. All but a small portion of the law school and police subjects were told that the principal character had been indicted for attempted kidnapping. Half of the subjects were given a bias by being told that he had previously been convicted for molesting children.

Several additional variables were in the pattern of the experiment. The control groups in each of the three populations were asked to write what they had seen and heard. Among the law students, there were also two groups who did the same, one, however, was told that they would be witnesses for the defendant, and another that they would be witnesses for the prosecution. In both the law and the police populations, a group was asked to leave the room and in another room, before the questionnaire was administered to them, they were given a brief talk by a status figure (see pp. 24-26) to see what influence he would have on their recall. Another group of law students and police trainees was taken to rooms where, instead of writing, they spoke into a tape recorder. There was also a group of law students and police trainees who were excused and asked to return a week later, when they were asked to write what they recalled of the picture. All those participating, whether reporting in writing, or orally, were asked a week later again to record what they had seen and heard. It was not possible to have more than a control group for the settlement house people because there was not a sufficient number who consistently attended the sessions.

At the end of the final session, one week after the picture was shown, each subject was given a post-questionnaire to fill out which asked specific questions concerning the film and which will be referred to later.

There were 115 possible items in the picture to be recalled.

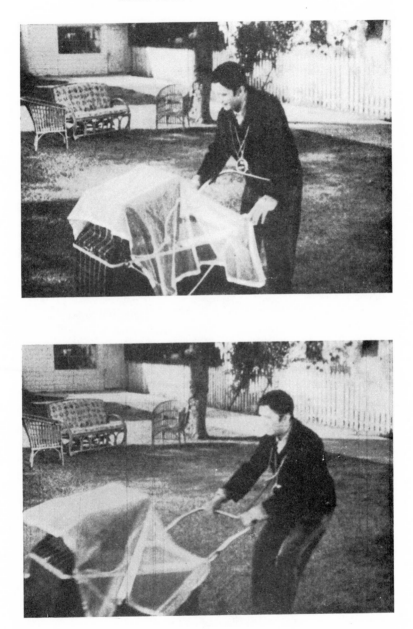

Reproduced with permission of the National Broadcasting Company.

Reproduced with permission of the National Broadcasting Company.

Reproduced with permission of the National Broadcasting Company.

We found that in each condition the higher the educational level, the more verbal were the subjects. This was obtained by a word count of the answers to the questionnaires which they filled out, in writing or orally, immediately after seeing the film. The Mean Word Count for each control group was: Law school 183, police trainees 163, settlement house 77.[158]

It was found that the mean number of items of correct recall and inferences reported are directly related to the amount of education of the subjects. Oral or written, the higher the educational standing of the group, the more items were recorded. Table "A" demonstrates this.

TABLE "A"

MEAN NUMBER OF ITEMS
CORRECTLY RECALLED AND INFERENCES

	Items of Correct Recall			Inferences		
	Law	Police	Settle-ment	Law	Police	Settle-ment
Control	15.2	9.5	5.3	6.8	5.8	4.8
Status-Influence	14.8	13.4	—	10.5	5.8	—
Second Week Only [159] . . .	13.8	9.0	—	7.2	6.2	—
Oral	12.2	8.0	—	5.2	5.6	—
Defense	12.2	—	—	7.1	—	—
Prosecution	15.3	—	—	5.8	—	—
TOTAL	14.0	10.3	5.3	7.2	5.8	4.8

When we discuss means there is, of course, some *overlap* of distribution among groups. There is no sharp line between them. While the mean correct recall for law students was 14.0, the highest single score for a police trainee was 22.0. The highest individual correct recall score for the settlement group was 13.0

---

[158] This represents a word count of reports made right after film presentation. This, therefore, represents the *maximum* number of words since the word count for the second week is lower. For the Settlement House the word count was based on an English translation for 12 of the 22 subjects who wrote their reports in Spanish — and the reports for 10 subjects who wrote in English. In translation, there was no appreciable difference in word count due to translation.

[159] Second Week Only is average recall a week after the picture was shown. This was the only written report that group wrote. The other means are the averages of reports for both weeks.

which is *higher* than the mean of about 10.0 for the police trainees but *below* the mean for the law students. The highest individual score for a law student was 23.0. This may not seem much better than the highest police trainee's score but there are many more law students who scored in the upper end of the range.

This trend of higher correct recall by those people of higher socio-educational status is supported by the mean correct recall of the 10 police trainees who had had some college education. Their mean score was about 14.0, which is significantly different than the mean of the police trainees, although not significantly different from that of the law students. A similar trend is evidenced by the settlement house people. One of them had some college, 9 had some high school, though it was questionable whether more than one had completed high school. Their mean recall score was about 6 whereas those who had only had some elementary schooling scored about 4.

It appears from Table "A" that *not only were there a higher number of items correctly recalled by those of higher educational status, but that there were more inferences, too, by those with more education.* If, however, we compare the proportion of the mean number of inferences to the mean number of items of correct recall, then we find that *the lower the educational status, the greater is the proportion of inferences to items of correct recall.* Whether stated in terms of over-all number of inferences or ratio of inferences to correct recall there would be a considerable degree of inaccuracy in testimony as to the event. The ratio of inferences to correct recall is illustrated by Table "B."

TABLE "B"

RATIO OF MEAN INFERENCE
TO MEAN ITEMS OF CORRECT RECALL [160]

	(N)	Law	(N)	Police	(N)	Settle-ment
Control	17	44.7%	21	61.0%	22	90.5%
Status-Influence	19	70.9%	22	43.3%	—	——
Second Week Only ...	19	52.2%	20	68.9%	—	——
Oral	15	42.6%	15	70.0%	—	——

[160] 100% would mean that there would be an equal number of inferences and correct recall.

	(N)	Law	(N)	Police	(N)	Settle-ment
Defense	20	58.2%	—	——	—	——
Prosecution	20	37.9%	—	——	—	——
TOTAL	110 [161]	51.4%	78 [161]	56.6%	22	90.5%

In testimony, if inferences are expressed in terms of perception, it is often not possible to distinguish fact from inference. To say, as some did, that the man in the picture was trying to stop the baby from crying, was a statement of recall based on two inferences: the first that there was a baby in the carriage because there was the sound of a baby crying and there was a baby carriage; the second inference built on this was that the man was rocking the baby carriage to quiet the baby. The second inference served to reinforce the first. In each case, the inference was founded on experience that baby carriage + crying baby = the accepted way of quieting a crying baby in a carriage; so, therefore, the man must be trying to quiet a crying baby.[162] In such a situation it cannot be stated as facts that there was a crying baby in the carriage and that the man was trying to quiet it by rocking the carriage.

In addition to correct recall of facts, there was also incorrect recall. The mean number of incorrect items and the ratio of such items to those correctly recalled is shown by Table "C.

TABLE "C"

MEAN NUMBER OF ITEMS INCORRECT ABOUT FACT
AND THEIR RATIO TO CORRECT RECALL
FOR ALL LAW, POLICE AND SETTLEMENT SUBJECTS
FOR BOTH WEEK 1 AND WEEK 2 COMBINED

Mean Number of Incorrect Recall Items			
Law	2.8	Settlement	1.6
Police	2.5	TOTAL	2.5

Ratio to Correct Recall Items			
Law	19.8%	Settlement	31.5%
Police	24.3%	TOTAL	21.9%

---

[161] Eighty-one other subjects among the law and police groups are not considered here but are considered on pp. 28-30, as they were given different instructions.

[162] See Hayakawa, *Meaning, Symbols and Levels of Abstraction*, in READINGS IN SOCIAL PSYCHOLOGY (Newcomb & Hartley eds. 1947).

There were also items recorded which were non-facts, *i.e.,* they were neither correctly nor incorrectly recalled, but stated as facts although not in the picture. It will be seen from Table "D," which gives the mean number of such non-facts and their ratio to facts correctly recalled, that they were not numerous.

TABLE "D"

MEAN NUMBER OF NON-FACT ITEMS AND THEIR RATIO TO CORRECT RECALL FOR ALL LAW, POLICE AND SETTLEMENT SUBJECTS FOR BOTH WEEK 1 AND WEEK 2 COMBINED

Mean Number of Non-Facts		Ratio to Correct Recall Items	
Law	0.6	Law	4.4%
Police	0.5	Police	4.6%
Settlement	0.2	Settlement	4.3%
TOTAL	0.5	TOTAL	4.5%

Table "E" indicates the ratio of the means of incorrectly recalled facts, non-facts, and inferences taken together to the means of correctly recalled facts for the three populations.

TABLE "E"

MEAN NUMBER OF INCORRECT RECALL ITEMS, NON-FACT, AND INFERENCES COMBINED AND THEIR RATIO TO CORRECT RECALL FOR ALL LAW, POLICE, AND SETTLEMENT SUBJECTS FOR BOTH WEEK 1 AND WEEK 2 COMBINED

Mean Number of Incorrect Recall, Non-Fact, and Inferences		Ratio to Correct Recall Items	
Law	10.6	Law	75.6%
Police	8.8	Police	85.5%
Settlement	6.6	Settlement	126.3%
TOTAL	9.5	TOTAL	81.4%

This table brings out in stark contrasts the high degree of erroneous "recall" by the three socio-educational groups. This would indicate that a witness may testify to a substantial proportion of "facts" which are not facts at all, and that the lower the socio-educational status of the witness the greater will be the inaccuracy of his testimony, assuming that his testimony is truthful as he perceives truth. It may be, however, that the better educated man will appear more reliable because he can better rationalize his perceptions and express such rationalizations more persuasively. This is brought out in an experiment conducted by Cantril. Six different poems were given to undergraduate students and each had the name of a supposed author. The names of three classical authors, Tennyson, Keats and Browning were ascribed to poems and the names of Edgar Guest and two "popular poets," one a "radio poet," were also included. All of the poems were by Shakespeare. The subjects were asked to rank them from 1 to 6, according to "literary merit." The "good" poets were ranked higher than the "poor" poets. A similar experiment with graduate students in English gave the same result but they gave "better reasons *why*" the poems were ranked as they were than did the undergraduates.[163]

Time Elapse

It is not infrequent that the question arises as to the duration of a happening or how long was the interval between two events. It has been shown that time is difficult to estimate accurately. (See Chapter I.) A week after our subjects had seen the picture and after they had made written or oral reports on their recall, they were asked how long the picture had taken. Immediately after the picture was shown, many of them exclaimed, "Is that all!" The subjects were not under stress when they made their estimates. But we do not usually estimate time while it is passing unless we are prepared to do so, and we rarely are. As participants in an accident or a crime, or as witnesses, our attention is not so much fixed on the elapse of time as on the event. As we shall see in Table "G," action items are the most frequently recalled. Our perception

---

[163] Cantril, *Experimental Studies of Prestige Suggestion*, 34 PSYCHOLOGY BULL. 528 (1937).

of the passage of time is generally a guess after the event. Table "F" shows the mean estimates made of the picture which had lasted 42 seconds.

TABLE "F"

MEAN ESTIMATES OF LENGTH OF PICTURE

Law	1 min. 58 sec.
Police	1 min. 28 sec.
Settlement	1 min. 32 sec.

It will be seen that all groups overestimated time and the law students significantly more than the other two groups.

Selectivity

In Chapter I, consideration is given to the phenomenon that perception and recall are selective. This, too, is illustrated by this study, for out of the 115 possible items to be perceived and recalled in the picture that was shown, the highest mean number correctly recalled was 16 by the status-influence group of law students immediately after the picture was shown. A week later in this group the mean number of items correctly recalled had diminished to about 14.

Selectivity also exists among different categories of items. Table "G" indicates the selectivity among items of action, person, background, and sound.

TABLE "G"

FREQUENCY OF CORRECT RECALL OF ITEMS OF ACTION, PERSON, BACKGROUND AND SOUND FOR EACH GROUP AND TOTAL MEANS FOR ALL GROUPS

	Law	Police	Settlement	Total Means
Action	7.29	4.95	2.64	5.91
Background	2.72	2.13	.50	2.25
Sound	2.45	2.16	1.68	2.26
Person	.99	1.09	.45	.96

It will be seen that action items were most frequently recalled by all population groups; and person items least frequently. Background and sound were about the same except for the settlement people who are relatively much better on sound items. The most frequently recalled item was the crying of the baby, which continued throughout most of the film. In action items, it was large movements more than small ones that were most frequently recalled. Thus, in testimony, it would appear that witnesses would be more accurate in describing gross acts and would tend to omit lesser actions, and as a result might distort the probative value of their testimony.

An analysis of the sound items recalled is also instructive with reference to testimony. Two women's voices were heard during the picture; only one of the women could be seen. Both voices were frequently mentioned in the answers, although in a number of cases the substance of what they said was merged and they were heard as if there had been only one speaker. However, the *content* of what was said was almost uniformly *inaccurate*. This corroborates the finding discussed in Chapter I that blanks in perceptions are filled in by the witness in conformity to his expectations. As Thucydides said, in reporting speeches, it was necessary "to make the speakers say what was in my opinion demanded of them by the various occasions...." [164]

Many a case, of course, turns on the precise language used in the situation. It would seem that testimony of precise language is extremely unreliable.

An illustration of such unreliability is dramatized by replies to questions asked the subjects in a post-questionnaire after they had recorded their recall the week after they had seen the picture. In the course of the picture, a woman's voice called out, "Mrs. Gerard, Mrs. Gerard, someone's running away with your baby." A young woman then ran out of the house shouting, "You bad boy! You bad boy!" The subjects were asked whether they thought the woman was the boy's grandmother, mother, a sitter, a sister, or a neighbor and why they thought so. Seventy percent of all subjects thought she was the mother. About a quarter of this three-quarters said

---

[164] THUCYDIDES, COMPLETE WRITINGS 14 (Modern Library ed. Crawley transl. 1951).

that they thought so because she had said, "My baby." No such words were used. Another 42% ascribed their conclusion to concern in voice, to her appearance or age. The other remaining 32% gave a variety of reasons such as "situation," and what "neighbor" said, etc.

Effect of Direct Questions

Thus, we find that in a situation similar to actual events testified to at a trial, only a small proportion of facts are recalled; and that witnesses report a high ratio of errors of fact, non-facts, and inferences. In a trial there is room for honest witnesses to differ as to items correctly perceived and recalled. There is also the probability that in all honesty they will testify as to erroneous perceptions, to matters that never were but are mistakenly recalled as perceptions, and to inferences derived from what had actually occurred. Each of these can in good faith be testified to as realities, for to the witness they appear real. As the result of his experience, they conform to his expectations as to what could or should have been present in the happening.

Because experience has indicated that there are omissions from any perception of what has occurred, lawyers have devised the processes of direct and cross-examination of witnesses to elicit a more complete account, to direct the attention of witnesses to perceptions not immediately recalled.[165] To test the effect of direct questioning after the recital of what had been recalled, a post-questionnaire addressed to specific items in the picture was administered. In other words, having considered free recall, what are the cueing effects of questions which are directed to specific items?

Three questions were asked concerning the appearance of the principal character in the picture. The questions and the summary of the answers follow:

"The man in the picture was dressed in (check one) a light jacket, dark jacket, wore no jacket."
The correct answer was that he wore a dark jacket. The *direct*

---

[165] We are not considering here the uses of cross-examination to uncover falsity.

question developed more correct recall of this item than the reports, written or spoken, immediately after viewing the picture and one week later, as is shown in Table "H." Most of the written and oral reports contained no mention of the jacket but about 22% of the police trainees described the jacket erroneously. In answer to the direct question, about 50% of the law students and police trainees were in error and 40% of the settlement house people.[166]

TABLE "H"

RESPONSES DESCRIBING JACKET WORN
BY PRINCIPAL CHARACTER

	Free Recall (Written and Oral Reports)			Direct Question (Multiple Choice)	
	Mentioned				
	% Correct	% Error	% No Mention	% Correct	% Error
Law	8.0	17.5	75.0	47.4	52.6
Police	6.5	22.5	71.0	49.1	50.9
Settlement	0.0	0.0	100.0	60.0	40.0

Almost no one mentioned in their written or oral reports that the man had sideburns. In answer to the *specific* question on the post-questionnaire, however, about 66% of the law students, about 74% of the police trainees, and 25% of the settlement people reported that he had sideburns. Nevertheless, among the law students, about 19% said he had a mustache and about 4% reported he had a crew cut. The remaining, about 9%, did not answer. For the police trainees these figures were respectively about 23%, 0%, and about 2%. Finally, for the settlement residents they were 35%, 5%, and 35%. It will readily be seen that in spite of better recall under direct presentation of alternatives a substantial number of individuals are either answering wrongly or sufficiently uncertain to make any guess at all. It should be noted that a small percentage of the latter may have omitted the answering due to sheer oversight. But even taking this into account, not much better than approximately two-thirds of all subjects answered correctly on

---

[166] See also ch. IV.

direct questions dealing with what was a perfectly clear and straightforward characteristic of the person in the picture.

The man's race was correctly identified when it was mentioned in the written and oral reports as well as in the answer to a direct question on the post-questionnaire.

A *direct* question in the post-questionnaire relating to action was as to a nonexistent fact. As the picture opened, the principal character lowered the mosquito net on the baby carriage. Nothing was taken out of the baby carriage at any time in the course of the picture. The question was, "At the beginning of the picture did you see the man place his hand in the baby carriage and take something out of it?" If the answer was "Yes," then the question was asked what he took out of the baby carriage and what he did with it. The answers are shown by Table "I."

TABLE "I"

AT THE BEGINNING OF THE PICTURE DID YOU SEE THE MAN PLACE HIS HAND IN THE BABY CARRIAGE AND TAKE SOMETHING OUT OF IT?

	% No	% Yes	% No Answer
Law	85.1	8.0	6.9
Police	78.9	19.3	1.8
Settlement	90.0	5.0	5.0

The striking feature of these responses is the percentage, particularly of police trainees, almost one-fifth of whom *perceived what had never happened.* These questions and the answers will be futher discussed when consideration is given to the effect of the status-influence figure.

In answer to the questions what the man had taken out of the carriage and what he had done with it, those who had perceived him taking something out replied "a bottle," "a rattle," or "a mirror." The object was said to have been put in his pocket, cradled in his arms, shaken, kept in his hands, put around his neck, etc. This is a clear case of the witness filling in the gaps in his recollection by inferences which would sustain his original perception or, as in this case, misperception.

The answers to these questions bear out Münsterberg's finding that "As to the influence of questions in the taking of testimony, the experiments demonstrate that the number of details which the memory produces can certainly be increased by questions, and, in some cases, even doubled. But the correctness and exactitude of the testimony decreases much more rapidly. This is to a certain degree the result of the hardly avoidable suggestive character of some of the questions." [167]

Another action question related to what the woman did as she came from the house. The post-questionnaire inquired whether she was: (a) carrying something in her hand; (b) waving her left arm with something in her hand; (c) waving her left arm with nothing in her hand; or (d) none of these. The correct answer was waving her left arm with nothing in her hand.

Only one person the first week and two persons the second, in their written or oral reports, mentioned the woman waving her hand. In answer to the *direct* question, however, only 20% of the law students, about 30% of the police, and 15% of the settlement house people gave the correct answer. The others either were wrong or made no response. This might appear to be a reasonable percentage of correct responses considering the fact that the arm movement was not an essential part of the action of the picture. However, these percentages of correct recall do not differ appreciably from what one could expect by chance, that is, guessing the answer without even having seen the film, where the guesser has one chance in four of being correct — a 25% chance.

In another question the subjects were directly asked, "How many people's voices did you hear?" Table "J" gives the replies.

TABLE "J"

ANSWERS IN PERCENTAGES TO DIRECT QUESTION ON POST-QUESTIONNAIRE ASKING SUBJECTS, "HOW MANY PEOPLE'S VOICES DID YOU HEAR?"

	1 Voice	2 Voices	3 Voices	"Unclear"	No Answer
Law	29.1%	46.8%	13.7%	3.6%	6.8%
Police	28.1%	49.1%	14.9%	0.0%	7.9%
Settlement	15.0%	20.0%	30.0%	0.0%	35.0%

---

[167] MÜNSTERBERG, PSYCHOLOGY: GENERAL AND APPLIED 401-02 (1915). But see Marshall, Marquis & Oskamp, fn. 189.

There were three voices — a crying baby and two women. It will be seen from Table "J" that less than one-fifth of the subjects heard correctly, except in the case of the settlement house people, 30% of whom heard three voices. While it might have been difficult for some to distinguish between the voice that called, "Mrs. Gerard, Mrs. Gerard, quick! Someone's running away with your baby" and the voice of the woman coming from the house who shouted, "You bad boy! You bad boy! ", which might lead to the inference by some that there was only one woman's voice, in view of the almost continuous crying of a baby (the most recalled item of all), the answer "one" voice was patently wrong. It is possible that there was semantic difficulty and that to some a baby's cry is not a "people's" voice. In a trial, this might have been cleared up by further direct questioning. It evidences a value of direct and cross-examination. However, in view of the answers to a subsequent question as to who the woman coming from the house was and the fact that about 63% of the law students answering the question, and about 80% of the police trainees answering the question, and 85% of the settlement house people answering the question said that the woman was the mother, it would indicate that the voices were distinguished but not recalled as separate voices (see discussion p. 16). This is a condensation, a merging process, "as though memory tries to burden itself as little as possible. For instance, instead of remembering two items, it is more economical to fuse them into one." [168]

The baby carriage was almost continuously in view; nevertheless, about 10% of the answers of all subjects to the *direct* question whether the hood was up or down or whether there was no hood were in error. The error for the law group was about 12%, for police about 8%, and for the settlement house about 11%. This was considered a background item (*i.e.,* neither action, personal, nor sound).

Another *direct* question concerning background was, "How many doors were there in the house? " And this was followed up by questions as to the difference between the doors, and whether they saw the woman go out of a door and, if so, which one. The correct answer was two doors, which was given by about 17% of

---

[168] Allport & Postman, *op. cit. supra* note 80.

the law students, about 32% of the police trainees, and 5% of the settlement house people. Here the police trainees scored notably higher than the others, but still only about one-third perceived the correct number of doors. (In the written and oral replies made immediately after the picture was shown and a week later, only one door was mentioned by 19% of the law students, 26% by the police trainees, and 6% by the settlement house people.) Thus, it will be seen that the police trainees did best, especially under direct questioning. Yet, only about 32% of the police trainees were accurate and about 67% were in error, which is not significantly better than would be expected by chance.

Status-Influence

What effect does status-influence have on recall? A witness is almost always affected by status-influence at some stage of trial. To many prospective witnesses the person who interviews them before they go on the stand is such a status figure. To almost all people a prosecuting attorney is, and it is a reasonable supposition that to all witnesses the judge at the trial has status-influence which affects them if for no other reason than that his status involves power. That is, he has the power to give approval which may be rewarding, and he has punitive power which may be threatening. Fromm suggests that "Even the picture of the judge, who, in democractic society, is elected and theoretically not above his fellow men, is tinged by the old concept of a judging god. Although his person does not carry any superhuman power, his office does. (The forms of respect due the judge are surviving remnants of the respect due a superhuman authority; contempt of court is psychologically closely related to lèse-majesté.)" [169] A judge's influence may also derive from his possible status as a reference figure, that is, a model to whose views and behavior another person attempts to adapt himself.

Immediately after showing the picture the experimenters asked a group of law students to go to a separate room with their law professor, and a group of police trainees to do the same with one of their instructors who was a police captain who wore his uniform

---

[169] FROMM, MAN FOR HIMSELF 235 (1947).

for the occasion, although generally he did not do so in the Police Academy. In both instances, the experimenters delayed going into the room to administer their questionnaires until the status figure, *i.e.,* the professor or the police captain, made the following statement:

> "It is extremely important that each of you gives us as much of his recollection as he possibly can, both as to what he heard and saw. I am particularly anxious that you do well in this. Very often it is found that the people answering the questionnaire omit simple things which may be important in a trial. For example, there was a tree on the lawn in front of the house. Or that at the very beginning the man put his hand in the carriage and took something out. Or in describing the house that the door on the right was partly open, or that the man, at the end, squatted under a mail box. It is all this kind of detail that we would like to have from you in so far as you can recall what you saw and heard."

A few minutes later an experimenter entered the room to distribute questionnaires. He did not remain in the room but the status figure did. The second week these (the status) groups remained in the same room with the other subjects to fill out their second questionnaires on their recall and the separate post-questionnaire.

No significant effect of status-influence was found in inducing recollection of the specific items or recording the non-facts mentioned by the status figure. However, as is shown by Table "K," the word count, the recall of facts, and the number of inferences were markedly affected and significantly different.

TABLE "K"

MEAN WORD COUNT, CORRECT RECALL AND INFERENCES FOR STATUS-INFLUENCE CONDITION IN LAW AND POLICE GROUPS AS COMPARED WITH THEIR CONTROL GROUPS

Word Count	Control	Status
Law	183	264
Police	135	178

Correct Recall	Control	Status
Law	15.2	14.8
Police	9.5	13.4

Inferences	Control	Status
Law	6.8	10.5
Police	5.8	5.8

Correct Recall and Inferences	Control	Status
Law	22.0	25.3
Police	15.3	19.2

It will be seen that for both law students and police trainees the effect of the status-influence person resulted in longer written reports. The effect of the status-influence person differed, however, with respect to each of the two groups: (1) the law student status-influence group made more inferences than did any other law or police group; and (2) the police trainee status-influence group had better recall than any other police group. (See Table "A.") As will be seen in Table "B" the ratio of inferences to correct recall was about 71% for the law students and about 43% for the police trainees in the status-influence condition.

The subjects in the status-influence condition had the same perceptual opportunity as those in the other conditions and each population group studied was of a different socio-educational status than the others. *This would imply that the quantity of matter recalled by a witness, the correctness of his recall and the proportion of his testimony that is inferential are dependent upon influences of others on him (not necessarily intentional influences), as well as upon his perception, his socio-educational status or other variables.*

Oral Reporting

Witnesses are rarely called to the stand without having previously made a statement, oral or in writing, to an attorney or investigator. It would appear that a written statement would bring out better recall.

This is borne out by Table "A" which reveals that those who reported orally as to what they had seen and heard recalled less and made fewer inferences than those who *wrote* their reports. (However, the law school group who were told they were for the defense were no different from the oral group in their recall.) When we consider the ratio of inferences to recall in the oral group (Figure 1), we find it to be about 70% for the police trainees and about 42% for the law students.

Furthermore, the question arises as to the reliability of recall by jurors in the jury room whose deliberations involve their oral restatement of the testimony to which they were witnesses. This might well be worthy of further research.

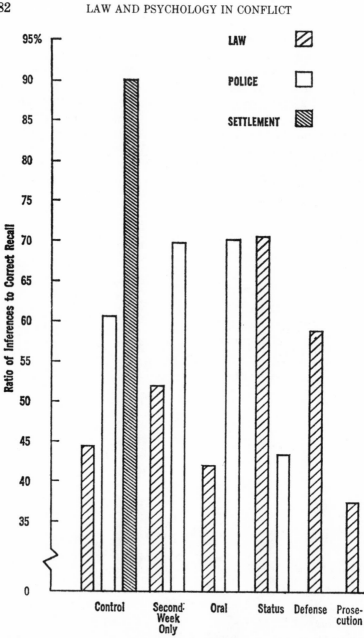

Figure 1. Ratio of Inferences to Correct Recall in Each Experimental Condition for Law, Police, and Settlement Groups.

In the case of the oral groups, there was some delay in the administration of the questionnaires before the subjects reported on tape. The first week the law students had to leave the hall where the picture was shown and go to another building, where they made their recordings in two shifts, the second shift more than half an hour after the picture was shown. The police trainees went to a different floor of the Police Academy and took turns using four recording instruments, which were all that were available. This meant a considerable delay before their recordings were completed. In both instances this delay might account for the lower percentage of correct recall in the oral than in the written reports.

Bias

"Now let's hear your distorted version."

Case and Comment, Jan.-Feb., 1965 at 18. Reprinted with permission.

It has been found that perception and recall are also dependent on the *bias* of the observer. Bias may determine attitude, which is similar to expectation in that it is a readiness for reinforcement. In this experiment, bias was introduced by informing half the subjects that the man in the picture who had been indicted for attempted kidnapping had previously been twice convicted for molesting children. No statistically reliable difference was found between the subjects who were given this biasing information and those who were not, either in the amount of correct recall or inferences made.[170]

However, although most of the subjects were informed that the principal character had been indicted, and that they would be called as witnesses, one group of 20 law students did not get this information. They had the highest correct recall of any of the law student groups (a mean of 16.10 items) and the lowest number of inferences (a mean of 4.90 items).[171] The difference cannot be dependent on the fact that they were not told they would be witnesses, because that variable was applied to other subjects and showed no statistically reliable effect. Was it then that not telling these subjects that the principal character was indicted caused them to feel no need to "take sides" and resulted in less stress? Does conscious or unconscious commitment to a party to litigation, or involvement in a process of fixing responsibility, placing blame, tend to reduce correct recall? Or does the mere fact of receiving no extraneous information enable one to recall more of a happening?

The result appears different, however, when there is reason to believe that the accused is *unsound mentally.* A group of 20 law students was given this bias by being informed that the principal character had been indicted for attempted kidnapping and that he "has a history of mental illness." Their mean correct recall was about 11%, the lowest of any of the law groups and their mean inferences were about 7%.[172] (Compare these figures to Table "A.")

Inferring from the fact that a person had been in a mental institution that he was a "mental case," the conclusion would follow that he was not fully responsible for his behavior and therefore did not intend to kidnap. As Heider said, ". . . if we are

---

[170] This does not prove that bias has no effect on recall, but may mean only that the biasing information given in this experiment was ineffective. See also experiments described in ch. V.

[171] A similar group of police trainees was too small to be statistically significant.

[172] While a similar group of police trainees indicated the same trend as to correct recall, their number was too small to be statistically significant.

convinced that *o* did *x* intentionally we generally link the *x* more intimately with the person than if we think that *o* did *x* unintentionally. By the same token, if we account for an act by a person's stupidity or clumsiness, that is, by ability factors, we tend to hold him less responsible than if we take the act as an indication of his motives." [173]

In such circumstances, facts which might or might not be felt to be relevant to inducing punitive action, such as holding a normal person responsible for his behavior, might appear irrelevant and be discarded if it was believed that the actor was after all a "mental case." To many people, moreover, mental illness is threatening to them and they would tend to avoid facts which they might feel would be descriptive of what they themselves might do.

Effect of Time on Recall

The decline in material recalled after a lapse of time, the slippage of memory, has already been discussed in Chapter I. As a result of the selective process, as has been shown, only a small proportion of the happenings were recalled immediately after viewing the picture. The decline or slippage of memory was not as great the following week. Perhaps the process of leveling and sharpening had slowed down. It would be interesting to know how much memory remained after one month or a year and whether over such greater intervals of time the rate of reduction would have increased or whether it had approached a point of decline at which the rate of change would become smaller and smaller. With one exception inferences also decreased. Would they have decreased further or increased with a greater lapse of time? We do not have the data to determine this.

Time elapse, however, between an occurrence and the need to recall it is only one factor in this phenomenon of forgetting. "For 'time' alone does not cause the forgetting . . . ." [174] Table "L" and Figure 2 not only show the deterioration of memory after one week but also indicate how *people differ in their recall under varied*

---

[173] HEIDER, THE PSYCHOLOGY OF INTERPERSONAL RELATIONS 112 (1958).

[174] Levine & Murphy, *The Learning and Forgetting of Controversial Material,* in READINGS IN SOCIAL PSYCHOLOGY 100 (Maccoby, Newcomb & Hartley 3d ed. 1958).

conditions. What happens is a process of leveling, sharpening, and assimilation which occurs not only in the progress of rumor but also in "the individual memory function as well." [175]

There is also a reduction in the number of inferences after the lapse of a week.

---

[175] Allport & Postman, *The Basic Psychology of Rumor,* in READINGS IN SOCIAL PSYCHOLOGY 64 (Maccoby, Newcomb & Hartley 3d ed. 1958).

TABLE "L"

MEAN NUMBER OF ITEMS OF CORRECT RECALL AND INFERENCES FIRST AND SECOND WEEKS

	Correct Recall Law		Correct Recall Police		Correct Recall Settlement		Inferences Law		Inferences Police		Inferences Settlement	
	W1	W2	W1	W2	W1	W2	W1	W2	W1	W2	W1	W2
Control	16.2	14.3	10.0	9.0	5.4	5.1	7.1	6.5	7.3	4.2	4.6	4.9
Status	16.0	13.5	13.8	13.0			12.0	9.0	6.7	5.0		
Week 2 only*		13.8		9.0				7.2		6.2		
Oral	12.4	11.9	8.1	7.9			5.6	4.9	6.2	5.1		
Defense	12.6	11.6					7.2	7.0				
Prosecution	15.9	14.7					6.4	5.3				
TOTAL	14.7	13.2	10.9	10.2	5.4	5.1	7.7	6.6	6.8	4.8	4.6	4.9

* Second Week Only: These groups only reported one week after seeing the picture.

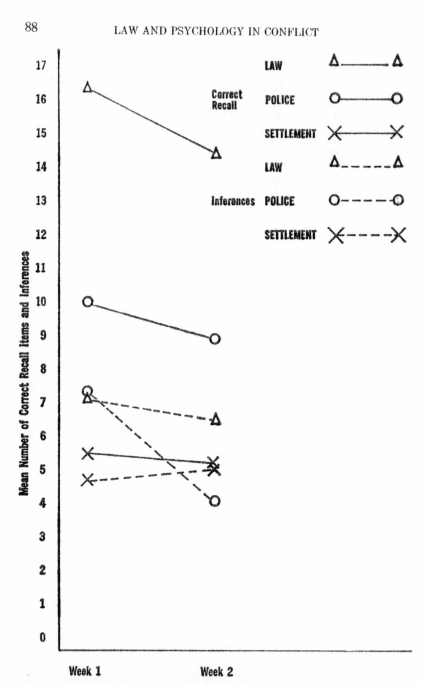

Figure 2. Mean Number of Correct Recall Items and Inferences During Week 1 and Week 2 for the Control Conditions in Each of the Law, Police, and Settlement Groups.

Some Effects of Punitiveness

This study examined the relative punitiveness of the three population groups and related punitiveness to recall. In a pre-test each subject was asked whether for each of ten crimes a person should be given psychiatric treatment or punished in one of seven different ways. He was first asked to give his choice of treatment or penalty for each crime for a first offender and then for one who had been previously convicted. The rating scale was scored 0 for psychiatric treatment and from 1 to 7 for punishment.[176] Figure 3 shows the consolidated punitiveness scores for all crimes for each socio-educational group, Figure 4 for murder.

---

[176] The choice of treatment or penalties was psychiatric treatment, fine, 1 year, 5 years, 10 years, 20 years or life imprisonment and death penalty. The crimes were stealing an automobile, using or possessing narcotics, selling any type of narcotic, assault with intent to kill, murder, having sexual intercourse with a girl under 16 years of age, gambling, rape, spying for another country and kidnapping.

Punishments for Ten Crimes

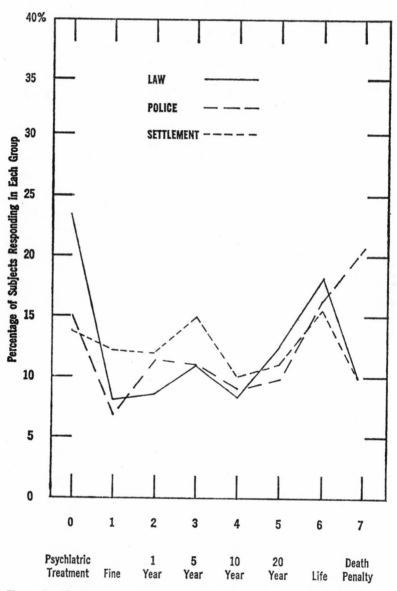

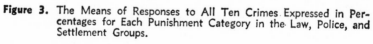

Figure 3. The Means of Responses to All Ten Crimes Expressed in Percentages for Each Punishment Category in the Law, Police, and Settlement Groups.

Punishments for Murder

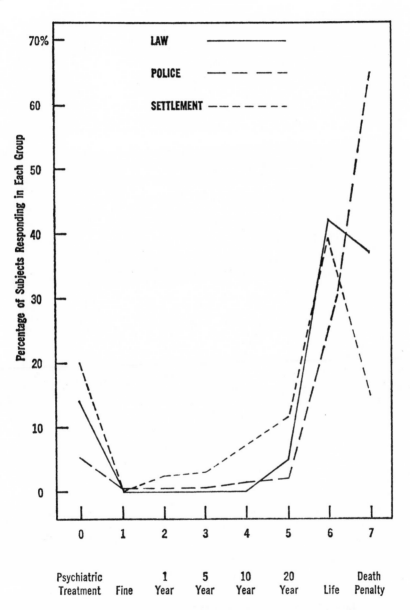

Figure 4. The Means of Responses to *Murder* Expressed in Percentages for Each Punishment Category in the Law, Police, and Settlement Groups.

The consolidated scores for all ten crimes indicate the following three most prevalent dispositions by each population group:

Law Students:
  18.6% for life imprisonment
  12.4% for 20 years imprisonment
  23.2% for psychiatric treatment

Police Trainees:
  17.0% for life imprisonment
  20.6% for death
  15.2% for psychiatric treatment

Settlement House:
  16.4% for life imprisonment
  14.8% for five years imprisonment
  14.3% for psychiatric treatment

Thus the death penalty was not one of the three most favored choices of the law students or settlement house people, but the most frequent choice of penalty (over one-fifth) by the police trainees.

Choice for each population group of a fine as punishment was:

Law Students 8.0%
Police Trainees 6.4%
Settlement House 12.0%

It will be noted that the settlement house people chose a fine more frequently than either of the two other population groups. We have no data to explain this. Possibly it was, because of their economic position, a fine seemed more serious to them; or they may have deemed the crimes for which they selected a fine less serious; or they might have been less punitive and concentrated more on the lower end of the scale.

Figure 4 dramatizes the differences in punitiveness among the three groups. It refers only to the punishments they would give for *murder.* Sixty-five percent of the police would give the death penalty as compared with about 41% of the law students and 17% of the settlement house people.

The median on the punitive scale (from 0 to 7) for the law

students was 3.41, for the police trainees 4.00, and for the settlement house people 3.39. It will be seen that the police trainees emerge with significantly higher scores on the punitive scale than the law students and settlement house people. The latter two groups do not differ from each other significantly.

The median split for punitiveness, combining all three groups, is 3.69. The percentage of each group above and below the combined median for punitiveness is shown in Table "M."

TABLE "M"

PERCENTAGE OF SUBJECTS IN EACH OF LAW, POLICE, AND SETTLEMENT GROUPS FALLING ABOVE AND BELOW THE MEDIAN ON PUNITIVE SCALE FOR ALL SUBJECTS TAKEN TOGETHER

	High Punitive	Low Punitive	Total Percent
Law	40.9%	59.1%	100.00
Police	67.3%	32.7%	100.00
Settlement	31.9%	68.1%	100.00

It appears clearly that about two thirds of the police trainees rank above the combined population punitive median and that the law students and settlement house people are relatively low. In other words, counting people in each group we find that the police trainees distribute themselves much more on the high end of the scale measuring "punitiveness."

Dividing each population group into high and low punitive (the high being above the median for each population, the low below the median on the ten crimes), it was found that *the above median subjects of each population had higher scores of correct recall than did the low punitive.* They also had higher scores for incorrect recall and lower scores for inferences, though neither of these was statistically significant. A comparison of the recall of high and low punitive subjects appears in Table "N."

TABLE "N"

PUNITIVENESS EFFECTS ON CORRECT RECALL
(SEPARATE MEDIANS FOR EACH GROUP)

	Punitive Groups	
	High	Low
Law	14.86	13.86
Police	11.83	9.86
Settlement	6.73	3.82
TOTAL	12.53	10.84

It is apparent that two independent variables affecting recall are present. While the mean recall of each socio-educational group is as shown in Table "A," *supra,* that is, the law students having best recall, then the police trainees and then the settlement house people, *within each socio-educational group, there is a significant difference between the high and low punitive in correct recall.*

The data of this experiment do not answer conclusively whether the greater punitiveness on the part of the police is due to a selective process by which men choosing police work tend to be more punitive, or more punitive applicants are selected as better fitting the model of what a policeman should be, or whether even after a short period in the Police Academy the trainees have adapted to a stereotype of a role which pictures a policeman as severe, hardboiled, and punitive. Selectivity and role may both be involved.

The police trainees showed *greater rigidity, i.e.,* unwillingness to lean backwards, than did the other populations studied. In answer to a question on the pre-questionnaire as to whether they would tend to lean backwards in a case where the penalty was more severe than where it was less severe, only 37% of the police trainees said yes, whereas 50% of the law students and 52% of the settlement house people replied in the affirmative. Again, whether this is the result of a selection process or role adaptation is uncertain.

Rigidity is one of the characteristics of the authoritarian personality. Another such personality characteristic is the response to authority.[177] The different effects of authority on law

---

[177] ADORNO, FRENKEL-BRUNSWICK, LEVINSON & SANFORD, THE AUTHORITARIAN PERSONALITY (The American Jewish Comm., Studies in Prejudice Series: Pub. No. 3, 1950).

students and police trainees appear in Table "K." The status-influence figure (a professor in the case of the law students and a police captain in uniform in the case of the police trainees) had the effect of producing half as many inferences by the police trainees as by the law students. The former, in response to the status figure's instructions, gave more correct facts than their control group and the same number of inferences, whereas there were no statistically different numbers of facts and substantially more inferences reported by the law school status-influence group than by their control group.

The answers to another question suggest the adaptation of police trainees to the policeman's role. This question was asked:

"Suppose that a trusted employee steals money from his employer on Monday. On Friday he returns the money and is caught when doing so. In your opinion, which of the following actions should be taken by the employer?"

Five answers were proposed and the subjects were asked to check one. The answers were:

"(1) Say nothing and forget the matter; (2) Bawl out the employee but do nothing further; (3) Transfer the employee to a job where he can't get his hands on money; (4) Report the matter to the police; or (5) Report the matter to the police and insist on prosecution."

Seventy-five percent of the law students, 79% of the settlement house people, and only 58% of the police trainees answered (2) or (3). However, 35% of the police checked answer (4) ("Report the matter to the police") compared with 8.8% of the law students and 9% of the settlement house people.

Another question revealed attitude differences between the law students and police trainees. They were asked:

"The law says that a person accused of a crime should be considered innocent until proven guilty. Still, it is said that where there is smoke there is likely to be some fire. It would probably be better, therefore, to assume that a person who is accused is likely to be guilty, but to give him the benefit of the doubt by adjusting the severity of the punishment. If there is some doubt, give him the mildest punishment possible for that crime. If there is no doubt about his guilt, give him the most severe punishment that the law prescribes for that crime.

"To what extent do you agree or disagree with the above statement? (Check one answer only.)

"(1) Agree very strongly; (2) Agree somewhat; (3) Can't decide; (4) Disagree somewhat; or (5) Disagree very strongly."

Eighty-two percent of the law students replied: "Disagree very strongly," but only 44% of the police trainees gave this response and 25% of them said either that they agreed very strongly or agreed somewhat, compared with less than 1% of the law students. (As 38% of the settlement house people answered, "Can't decide," it appeared that the question probably was too difficult for them and so their replies are not considered here.) This too may be a case of adaptation to the expectations of role, the law students accepting the principle of Anglo-American law that a man is innocent until proven guilty and a large proportion of the police trainees suspecting the accused and preferring to give him some punishment if there is doubt as to his guilt. "Since the police officer obtains his rewards and satisfactions from the successful identification of persons responsible for misconduct, and since such success is 'confirmed' through prosecution, conviction and sentencing, any interference with this sequence may be experienced as terribly frustrating."[178]

As policemen are frequently witnesses, the quality of their testimony is important. Their greater tendency toward punitiveness than that of the other two population groups referred to and their greater rigidity have been mentioned. Toch and Schulte

---

[178] Toch, *Psychological Consequences of the Police Role,* a paper presented at the Annual Meeting of the American Psychological Association, September 1, 1963. See also Allport & Postman, *The Basic Psychology of Rumor,* in READINGS IN SOCIAL PSYCHOLOGY 54, 63, 65 (Maccoby, Newcomb & Hartley 3d ed. 1958). They showed to a group of police officers a picture involving police and a night stick. In the account of the picture by the police officers, "The entire reproduction centered around the police officer (with whom the subjects undoubtedly felt keen sympathy or 'identification'). Furthermore, the night stick, a symbol of their power, ... becomes the main object of the controversy. The tale as a whole is protective of, and partial to, the policeman." This reaction is, of course, not peculiar to the police. Allport and Postman mention a picture "containing women's dresses, as a trifling detail," which in the telling became "a story exclusively about dresses."

found that advance police administration students *perceive more violence* in a situation than do first-year police administration students or students in their first year of psychology. In their experiment, Toch and Schulte showed their subjects nine stereograms which simultaneously presented to one eye a picture of a crime being committed (violence) and to the other a neutral picture. The advance students saw twice as many violent pictures as did the first-year police students and more than twice as many as the psychology students. Toch and Schulte say that, "Given a task in which others predominantly perceive non-violent content, subjects with police schooling have become relatively aware of violent content." "This does not mean," they tell us, "that the law enforcer necessarily comes to exaggerate the prevalence of violence. It means that the law enforcer may come to accept crime *as a familiar personal experience,* one which he himself is not surprised to encounter. The acceptance of crime as a familiar experience in turn increases the *ability* or readiness to perceive violence where clues to it are potentially available."[179] It may, however, be another function of punitiveness.

Why do the more punitive people tend to have greater correct recall? Freyberg investigated a series of "variables that enter into interpersonal decision-making and that may lead to the perception that another desires to increase his power in a relationship." He suggests that the subjects of his experiment had greater recall of the arguments of another person who was pitted against them when they "had grounds for suspecting the veracity of *C's* [the other person's] expressed opinions." [180] This would mean that if the more punitive people felt their sense of power threatened they would be more alert to threatening situations, that their sensitivity to their environment and to happenings would be sharpened.

It would seem that people who are extra-punitive would tend to look outside of themselves for cues, because they would want to place the blame outside of themselves and not look into their own punitiveness, whereas people who are intra-punitive would look for blame in themselves as well as outside. This would consume more

[179] Toch & Schulte, *Readiness to Perceive Violence as a Result of Police Training,* 52, 4 BRITISH J. PSYCHOLOGY 389, 391-92 (1961).
[180] Freyberg, *The Effect of Mistrust in Interpersonal Decision-Making on*

energy and therefore would leave them less energy to pursue the extraneous facts than that available to the extra-punitive persons.

Extra-punitiveness can be conceived as a projection of one's own faults and weaknesses onto others. This would require the extra-punitive to look outward for situations appropriate to such projection, situations in which they could safely project faults and weaknesses onto others without invoking punitive authority towards themselves. Responding to persons with status-influence or testifying for the prosecution or prescribing severe punishments for social deviants might be appropriate situations. Thus the extra-punitive are in greater need than the intra-punitive to have information about their environment to determine (mostly unconsciously) when they can safely reduce the tensions of their motives without exposing themselves to retribution.[181]

These findings concerning punitiveness do not mean that in all situations these socio-educational groups would show the same relative punitiveness or hostility. It is probable that punitiveness is a function of situation as well as socio-educational status. In other words, if other questions had been put to them the settlement house people might have proven more punitive, but they were less punitive in considering punishments which the law might inflict because of their own frequent involvement with the law. It is clear that they have more trouble with the police, for example, than do the other groups of the population.[182]

Table "O" shows the replies to the question: "What experience have you had with the police that you think was fair or unfair?

Hostility (unpublished Doctoral Dissertation, Grad. School of Arts and Science, (N.Y.U. (1962)).

[181] ADORNO, FRENKEL-BRUNSWICK, LEVINSON & SANFORD, *op. cit. supra* note 177 at 409-11; SARNOFF, PERSONALITY DYNAMICS AND DEVELOPMENT 150 (1962).

[182] And the police have different attitudes toward them than to middle-class people. Toch, *Psychological Consequences of the Police Role, supra* note 178.

Please write below what this experience was."

TABLE "O"

"UNFAIR," "FAIR," AND "NOT ANSWERED"
EXPERIENCES WITH POLICE

	N Unfair	X	%	X Fair	%	X No Answer	%
Law	184	30	16.3	17	9.2	137	74.5
Police	125	6	4.8	9	7.2	100	88.0
Settlement	51	15	29.4	3	5.9	33	64.7

N = Number Subjects Overall
X = Number of Subjects in the Category
% = Percent of Subjects in the Category of Over-all (Total) Number

It is clear that the settlement house people have the most complaints, more than the law students and the police trainees. The complaints are significantly different from each other. One of the police trainees criticized the police with the entertaining account of the following incident:

"I once found something (a wallet) and turned it in to the police precinct. They did not even thank me. I was rather annoyed."

Most of the law students' complaints dealt with traffic tickets although one law student complained of illegal searches by the police of all teen-agers in the neighborhood "just because it had a high delinquency rate." The settlement house people, on the other hand, had more serious complaints, such as the following:

"On one occasion two detectives impounded my husband's automobile without any reason or proof. They claimed that he was selling dope (pusher) and narcotics. After an argument of several minutes the detectives withdrew because they could not find anything that would justify their insinuations [charge]. This was natural and to be expected because my husband is a man who never had problems before with the police. He always lived honorably from his work. I thought this was a scandal — and our neighbors intruded themselves into this and caused us great humiliation. The police barged into our house and humiliated us in front of the neighbors."

There are certain related trends apparent in this data: high punitive people and those assuming the role of witnesses for the prosecution have greater correct recall than do low punitive people, people assuming the role of witness for the defendant, and those who believe that an indicted defendant is mentally ill. It would appear, then, that the high punitive people and witnesses for the prosecution are more aggressively motivated than the others. This would indicate that recall is a function of aggressive motivation, at least within each socio-educational population group.

Just as we have no data indicating a relationship between intelligence and correct recall, so, too, our data does not indicate that there is a difference in intelligence between high and low punitive people, though the former have better correct recall.

In summary, where there is a greater verbal capacity, there is greater correct recall and there are a greater number of inferences but a lower ratio of inferences to correct recall. Within each socio-educational group, where there is high punitiveness, there is greater recall and less where there is low punitiveness. When a status figure urges subjects to do well there is a greater number of inferences by law students and less by the police trainees than by their control groups. Among the law students, those who were told that they would be witnesses for the prosecution had greater recall than those who were told that they would be witnesses for the defendants. (See Tables "A," "B," and "L.")

For the trial lawyer and the court this would imply that the accuracy of recall does not stand alone but is related to such variables as socio-educational status, role, and personality factors, such as punitiveness. At the present state of the law, there is little that a trial court can do to relate accuracy of recall to those variables. Do these phenomena not, however, present a challenge to lawyers and judges to stimulate and participate in research to test new judicial practices that might produce greater objective reality in testimony, that might produce greater correspondence between what is perceived and recalled by those who testify (their subjective reality) and what is objectively real? Do we not need to be able to identify those factors that bear upon differences in the recall of witnesses for the plaintiff or prosecution and for the defendant, and witnesses who react differently to various influences?

CHAPTER IV

EXAMINATION OF WITNESSES

> "Be thorough in the examination of
> witnesses, and be heedful of your
> words, lest through your words the
> witnesses be led to testify falsely."[183]

The examiner of witnesses may use various techniques and a number of tones. He may be direct, severe, considerate, sly, ironical, bombastic, hostile, supportive, etc. He may want to bring out facts. He may want to obfuscate. His method and purpose may be to destroy the credibility of the witness or his testimony.

Possibly the most devastating cross-examination of a would-be expert was that conducted of Job by the Lord. Job had been accused by one Elihu: "But Job doth open his mouth in vanity; he multiplieth words without knowledge."[184]

Then the Lord took over.[185] His first question was humiliating. The technique was described as "out of the whirlwind." Not many lawyers can achieve this devastating capacity. "Who is this that darkeneth counsel by words without knowledge?" The second question was a sockdolager and opened Job's ignorance to all. "Where wast thou when I laid the foundations of the earth? Declare, if thou hast the understanding. Who determined the measures thereof, if thou knowest?" etc.

Question after question was asked that the witness failed to answer. Finally, after several chapters and verses the witness was completely broken. He caved in. He had failed and he declared: "Behold, I am of small account; what shall I answer Thee? I lay my hand upon my mouth. . . . I know that Thou canst do every thing, And that no purpose can be withholden from Thee. . . . Therefore have I uttered that which I understood not, Things too wonderful for me, which I knew not."[186]

---

[183] Simeon Ben Shatach in the TALMUD, *Mishnah Avot* 1, 9.
[184] BOOK OF JOB, ch. 35, verse 16.
[185] Chs. 38 and 39.
[186] Ch. 40, verse 4 and ch. 42, verses 2 and 3.

Technique and tone of examination have an importance in connection with the accuracy and completeness of recall. Kent H. Marquis,[187] Stuart Oskamp[188] and the author conducted research into these problems.[189]

We began with common assumptions such as:

1. That the accuracy and completeness of testimony will be higher when the examination is conducted in a supportive atmosphere rather than in a challenging one;

2. That as the degree of specificity of questioning increases, the range of completeness would increase somewhat but the accuracy greatly decline;

3. That leading questions would produce less accurate and complete testimony than that obtained by non-leading questions; and

4. That leading questions asked in a supportive atmosphere would produce most errors.

To our surprise substantially none of these four hypotheses was sustained.

We prepared a moving picture with a sound track which we showed to our witnesses before questioning them. The picture lasted about two minutes, and the contents were as follows:

"Two college-age boys are seen throwing a football. The camera pans from them, showing a large building and parking lot and stops at the doorway of a supermarket from which several people emerge. A young man and woman carrying packages and engaged in conversation come from the doorway and walk behind a row of cars. The man says he forgot to get something and leaves. The woman continues walking and is

---

[187] Study Director, Survey Research Center, Institute for Social Research, University of Michigan. Ph.D., Social Psychology, University of Michigan, 1967.

[188] Professor of Psychology, Claremont Graduate School. Ph.D., Stanford, 1960.

[189] Marshall, Marquis & Oskamp, *Effects of Kind of Question and Atmosphere of Interrogation on Accuracy and Completeness of Testimony*, HARV. L. REV. 1620 (May 1971); and Marquis, Marshall & Oskamp, *Testimony Validity as a Function of Question Form, Atmosphere, and Item Difficulty*, J. APPLIED SOCIAL PSYCHOLOGY 167-86 (1972).

struck by a car backing out of the parking line. She loses hold of her package and falls to the pavement. The car stops; the driver gets out, approaches the woman and says, "Don't you ever watch where you're going?" The woman gets up and swears at him. Her companion returns running and shouts something. A scuffle ensues between the companion and driver. The companion is pushed to the pavement, spilling the contents of his package. The boys who played football earlier in the picture appear, ask what happened, and restrain the men. One of the boys trots off in the direction of the supermarket entrance saying he will call the police." [190]

There were a total of 151 "witnesses" in our experiment, all males between 21 and 64 years of age. We obtained them from the Fire Department of Ann Arbor, Michigan, and several local community service clubs. They were neither very poor, very rich, nor educationally deprived. After the film was shown the experimenter told them that they were to consider themselves witnesses to the events shown in the film, and that he wanted to find out everything that they had witnessed, that is, everything they had seen or heard in the film. And they were asked to tell the truth, the whole truth and nothing but the truth. Each witness was then asked to report what he had seen and heard, and the answers were taped.

Type and Atmosphere of Interrogation

Following this free report the witnesses were divided into four groups. Each group was then interrogated in one of the following modes: (a) by moderate guidance; (b) by high guidance; (c) by structured multiple choice questions; and (d) by structured leading questions. Examples of questions in each type of interrogation are shown in Table 1.

---

[190] While we were filming a woman in the parking lot seeing the scuffle and hearing the boy saying he would call the police exclaimed: "Well I would think you should!"

Table 1

Examples of Questions from Each Type of Interview

Question Number	Open-ended Questions		
	Moderate Guidance	Question Number	High Guidance
2	Now describe the area you saw at the *very beginning of the film*, that is, to the right of the main building: what was the setting, what was the background, what objects were visible, where were they located, what color were they, and so forth.	2	Tell me about the traffic and weather conditions.
		3	Mention in detail, everything about the main building you saw.
		4	How many signs did you see, where were they, and what did they look like?
	PROBE: Now tell me *other* details you can remember about the setting at the very beginning of the film, that is, the area to the right of the main building: the background, the objects present, their locations, their colors, etc.	5	How many houses, if any did you see? Describe them in detail.
		6	If you saw any other buildings, tell me everything you know about them.
		7	Describe everything else you saw to the right of the main building.

Question Number	Structured Questions		
	Multiple Choice	Question Number	Leading
1	Where did the incidents happen: in a vacant lot, in a street, on a sidewalk, in a parking lot, or some place else?	1	The events you saw took place in a street, didn't they?
		2	There were cars in the area?
2	Was the parking lot you saw empty or were there cars in it?	3	A boy collecting shopping carts was visible at some time?
3	Was there a boy collecting shopping carts visible at any time or wasn't such a boy visible at any time?	5	It was a *football* that the people were playing with, wasn't it? (IF NOT FOOTBALL, ASK:) What kind of ball were they playing with?

Structured Questions —Cont'd

Question Number	Multiple Choice	Question Number	Leading
5	Several witnesses have stated that some people were playing with a ball. What kind of ball was it: football, basketball, volley-ball, baseball, or something else?	9	There was a sign with red lettering in the front window of the building wasn't there?
9	What color was the lettering on the sign in the front window of the building: red, blue, green or was it some other color?		

Half of the witnesses in each group were interrogated in a supportive atmosphere and half in a challenging atmosphere. Although the challenged witnesses were more inclined to feel that the interrogator thought poorly of their performance and they showed a tendency to have a less favorable self-perception of their capabilities as witnesses, and were more inclined than the supported witnesses to believe the interrogator wanted biased answers, *the experimental atmospheres had no important effect either on the accuracy or completeness of testimony.* See Tables 2 and 2A.

Table 2

AVERAGE ACCURACY AND COMPLETENESS INDEX SCORES FOR PRESENT ITEMS BY INTERROGATION ATMOSPHERE AND TYPE OF QUESTION [6]

TYPE OF QUESTION	ACCURACY INDEX		COMPLETENESS INDEX	
	Supportive	Challenging	Supportive	Challenging
Free Report	96		28	
Moderate Guidance	89	90	49	46
High Guidance	86	87	58	54
Multiple Choice	83	80	80	87
Leading	79	83	84	84

Table 2A

Type of	Percentage Increase in:	
Question	Completeness Index Score	Accuracy Index Score
Moderate Guidance	71	−06
High Guidance	100	−10
Multiple Choice	200	−15
Leading	200	−16

Note.—The percentage increase is computed as: (Interview Score minus Free Report Score) divided by Free Report Score.

The very act of interrogation and type of questions asked had, as we had expected, a marked positive effect on completeness. Contrary to our initial hypotheses, they had very little effect on accuracy. *It should be noted here that the type of memory required of the witnesses was crucial.* That is, when the questions called for recognition, as did the multiple choice and leading questions, rather than memory, coverage increased much more than accuracy decreased. Comparing the high guidance supportive questioning, the type in our experiment most closely resembling direct examination, with the leading challenging questioning, which was closest to cross-examination, reveals a decrease in accuracy of only three percentage points accompanied by a gain in coverage of twenty-six percentage points. The free reports were substantially less complete than the responses to any form of interrogation.

This accords with Luh's classic result to the effect that reporting of previously learned nonsense syllables is better under *recognition than recall procedures.* When an interrogator employs recognition procedures he reduces the amount of information that the subject must process to answer each question.[191]

Interrogation appeared to focus the witness's attention and thus stimulate his recall.

Legally Relevant Items in Picture

Of the 884 scorable items to be recalled, 130 were classified as legally relevant to a suit for damages for personal injury or an indictment for assult. These items were selected by several

---

[191] See generally, *The Conditions of Retention,* 31 PSYCHOLOGICAL MONOGRAPHS No. 3 (1922) (Monograph 142).

experienced trial lawyers. We found that, except in the free report, legally relevant items were mentioned with slightly less accuracy than legally irrelevant items. On the other hand, there was greater completeness in the coverage of legally relevant items. See Table 3.

Table 3

AVERAGE ACCURACY AND COMPLETENESS INDEX
SCORES FOR PRESENT ITEMS BY TYPE
OF QUESTION AND LEGAL RELEVANCE 10

TYPE OF QUESTION	ACCURACY INDEX		COMPLETENESS INDEX	
	Relevant	Not Relevant	Relevant	Not Relevant
Free Report	97	95	34	22
Moderate Guidance	88	92	55	40
High Guidance	85	90	64	45
Multiple Choice	79	84	87	81
Leading	78	84	88	80

Salience of Items in Picture

By pre-testing we also selected items that were more salient as compared with items less salient.[192] Some items are more likely to be recalled spontaneously than others, that is, are more salient than others to the viewer or hearer. Our hypothesis, that with increasing specificity of questioning coverage increases somewhat and accuracy greatly declines, was borne out with respect to low salient items; but only to a small degree with high salient items.[193]

---

[192] "On the basis of the pretest information, each scored item was assigned to one of five categories representing the probability that the item was mentioned by pretest witnesses (high school students and members of the staff of the Survey Research Center) spontaneously in a 'free report' condition. The probability categories used were: .00, .01 to .12, .13 to .25, .26 to .50, and .51 to 1.00."

[193] This apparently accounts for the differences between our results and those of other studies concerning the effects of specific questioning. Most other studies asked specific questions about nonsalient facts. Their finding that interrogatory testimony produces a great deal of error and only slightly more coverage was really due not to the effect of questioning per se but to the difficulty of the items which were the subject of the interrogation. Our data indicated that for moderately and very salient items, specific questioning greatly expands the amount of material covered with little or no loss of accuracy.

Putting it differently, our experiment indicated the structured questions made recall easier and high salience items by definition could be recalled more easily than low salience items. This is illustrated by Table 4.

Table 4

AVERAGE ACCURACY AND COMPLETENESS INDEX SCORES FOR PRESENT ITEMS BY TYPE OF QUESTION AND SALIENCE

TYPE OF	SALIENCE CATEGORY				
QUESTION	.00	.01-.12	.13-.25	.26-.50	.51-1.00
Accuracy Index					
Free Report	100	99	94	95	99
Moderate Guidance	72	96	79	94	98
High Guidance	58	94	74	89	98
Multiple Choice	61	78	81	83	98
Leading	56	80	80	85	96
Completeness Index					
Free Report	01	06	14	40	70
Moderate Guidance	13	24	45	67	84
High Guidance	20	46	50	69	88
Multiple Choice	64	81	82	92	98
Leading	66	77	84	92	98

Both in regard to accuracy and completeness our witnesses were able to testify with impressive ability. For instance, those confronted with leading interrogation in a challenging atmosphere testified with approximately 83% accuracy and 84% coverage. (See Table 2.) Part of the success of their performance must be attributable to the short time interval between their seeing the movie and being interrogated. This does not occur in actual cases. A period of days, even weeks or months, intervenes between the event and the statement obtained from the witness by counsel or investigator; and an even longer time before testimony is given in court. Nevertheless, despite the effect of the time interval on overall performance, we believe that our findings as to the nature of the *relationship* between the specificity of interrogation and the accuracy and completeness of testimony would not have been disturbed had we allowed a greater time interval. In fact, over a greater interval, the stimulating effect interrogation has on recall might have been even more pronounced. Further study of this phenomenon would, of course, be worthwhile.

Changes in Testimony

It is common for a witness to make a statement about an event shortly after it has occurred. Later, in court, his testimony may be substantially more complete than the earlier statement. The two statements may even be inconsistent. Both such variances are apt to occasion an attempt by opposing counsel to cast aspersions on the witness's recollection or honesty. However, our data indicate that the very act of interrogation tended to produce much greater completeness of recall. In addition we found that the more accurate witnesses were often those who after interrogation said that they wanted to change the testimony that they had given in their free reports. In other words, their interrogation apparently caused them to reconsider or reevaluate their earlier statements. This is supported by a finding by Buckhout that "The good witnesses also expressed less confidence than witnesses who impeached themselves."[194] Nevertheless, they tend to be good game for gunning by the cross-examiner.

In *United States v. Rappy*[195] Learned Hand, J. reminds us: "Anything may in fact revive a memory: a song, a scent, a photograph, and allusion, even a past statement known to be false."

Our finding, that those witnesses who wished to change their testimony tended to be more accurate than others, supports the belief of a highly respected psychiatrist that complete consistency in testimony is likely to be a sign of perjury.[196] Thus attacks on

---

[194] Buckhout, *Eyewitness Testimony*, 231 (No. 6) SCIENTIFIC AMERICAN 28-31 (1974).

[195] 157 F.2d 964, 967 (1946).

[196] Kubie, *Implications for Legal Procedure of the Fallibility of Human Memory*, 108 U. PA. L. REV. 59, 67 (1959).

the integrity of a witness whose courtroom testimony is more complete than an earlier statement, may be irrelevant and even improper. They raise a caveat against the conventional assumption that a change of testimony indicates unreliability or even perjury.[197]

We should note some differences between our experiment and courtroom processes. With respect to coverage, if on direct examination a witness failed to mention a legally important item counsel undoubtedly would probe further. Such a practice would make direct examination more like our structured interrogation, where leading rather than open-ended questions were used. Consequently, this should tend to lessen the difference in coverage between the two types of interrogation.

In interviewing, where information sought is to be aggregated for statistical purposes, it may matter very little that a single interviewee is inaccurate on any specific item. However, in a trial such inaccuracy might seriously affect the result. For example, suppose a witness testified that in our movie the driver had sounded his horn before backing out. Such testimony would change the whole weight of evidence in an action for negligence. So it is by no means clear that an interrogation procedure eliciting much more coverage at the expense of little more error is to be preferred to one that produces less inclusive but more accurate testimony. It is a complex value judgment to what extent "the whole truth" should weigh against "nothing but the truth."

Stress

We have already discussed the effect of stress on perception. Stress may have a different effect on recall or task performance. Münsterberg has suggested that moderate stress improves while little stress and great stress reduce the quality of performance.[198]

---

[197] The rule that generally a prior written statement cannot be used to corroborate testimony, though it may be used by him to refresh his memory, is not involved.

[198] Münsterberg, ON THE WITNESS STAND: ESSAYS IN PSYCHOLOGY AND CRIME, (1923).

A number of studies have shown how stress may affect testimony.[199]

It has also been found that performance of some tasks was improved when the subjects of the experiment believed others were evaluating their performance.[200] This phenomenon differed in our experiment from that which would be present in a courtroom in which a witness is surrounded by friends, enemies and "peers," all of whom are evaluating him and before whom he does not wish to appear foolish or inconsistent. Considerable research is necessary to determine the relationship of accuracy and coverage to the stress of a witness and whether, for example, to achieve the best performance, the type of interrogation might be tailored to the witness's initial degree of stress and to the salience of the items questioned.

There is a movement these days towards permitting press and television cameras in courtrooms. (A few courts have already permitted this.) What stress may be created by these? What would be the effect of such stress on the performance of witnesses, the accuracy and completeness of their testimony, their need to appear consistent, perhaps their desire to be histrionic? Considerable research is needed before these questions can be answered, and it would seem proper that they be answered tentatively at least, if not definitely, before cameras are permitted to intrude at a trial.

Reinforcement and Bias

Questions arise also with respect to our findings that there was no difference between the effects of a supportive and a challenging atmosphere of interrogation. Our hypothesis that the bias of a supportive interrogation with leading questions would produce most errors was not sustained. But suppose, instead of an interrogation for a short period, it had continued for a day or two

---

[199] Driver, *Confessions and the Social Psychology of Coercion,* 82 HARV. L. REV. 42, 46-47 (1968); Foster, *Confessions and the Station House Syndrome,* 18 DE PAUL L. REV. 683, 684-93 (1969).

[200] Henchy & Glass, *Evaluation Apprehension and the Social Facilitation of Dominant and Subordinate Responses,* 10 J. PERS. & SOC. PSYCHOLOGY 446 (1968); Zajonc, *Social Facilitation,* Technical Report 30, (1965), Prepared for Office of Navy Research, Inst. for Soc. Research, U. of Mich.

days. Perhaps the effect on a witness of support or challenge might be different.

In our supportive interrogations the interrogator gave neither positive nor negative contingent reinforcement. That is, he did not approve or disapprove of specific answers or of answers on a particular subject. The same atmosphere was maintained throughout regardless of the answers to specific questions. Contingent reinforcement, however, has been found to be crucial to a change of performance.[201]

Some studies have shown that interviews systematically using positive reinforcement increase both the amount and validity of information reported. [202] Other studies have shown that reinforcement can decrease validity by biasing the recall of the subject [203] and inducing him to believe his own biased statements. This has frequently taken place after a false confession.[204]

To appear consistent and convincing a witness may trap himself by a previous false or erroneous statement, by a bias he has assumed or into which he has been pressured.

In our study the witnesses did not come to testify with a bias. They had neither motive for taking sides nor for lying. As indicated in Chapter I, there are emotionally disturbed persons and those with an extreme desire for ego-enhancement who claim to have seen, heard or participated in events that never happened or did not take place in their presence. No such situation existed, of course, in our experiment.

However, even a mild exaggerator, while attempting to prevent falsity in his testimony from becoming apparent, may vary his

[201] Truax, *Reinforcement and Nonreinforcement in Rogerian Psychotherapy*, 71 J. ABNORMAL & SOCIAL PSYCHOLOGY 1 (1966).

[202] Marquis, Cannell, & Laurent, *An Experimental Study of Effects of Reinforcement, Question Length, and Reinterviews on Reporting Selected Chronic Conditions in Household Interviews*, VITAL & HEALTH STATISTICS (1972).

[203] Greenspoon, *The Reinforcing Effect of Two Spoken Sounds on the Frequency of Two Responses*, 68 AMERICAN J. PSYCHOLOGY 409 (1955); Hildum & Brown, *Verbal Reinforcement and Interviewer Bias*, 53 J. ABNORMAL & SOCIAL PSYCHOLOGY 108 (1956); Taffel, *Anxiety and the Conditioning of Verbal Behavior*, 51 J. ABNORMAL & SOCIAL PSYCHOLOGY 496 (1955).

[204] Bem, *Inducing Belief in False Confessions*, 3 J. PERSONALITY & SOCIAL PSYCHOLOGY 707 (1966); Zimbardo, *The Psychology of Police Confessions*, PSYCHOLOGY TODAY, Vol. 1, No. 2, 16-20, 25-27, June 1967.

testimony in areas peripheral to his initial falsehood. The person who lies in the presence of cues associated with telling the truth may blur the truth in his own mind and may actually come to believe his false statement.[205] And when a witness is positively and contingently reinforced by interrogation, it may enhance this process of self-delusion.[206]

The fact that our witnesses lacked bias is relevant to the issue of whether counsel shall be allowed to ask leading questions of his witness. Our data indicate that from a testimonial point of view there might be little value in the rule that prevents leading questions to one's own witness. However, in a trial where parties are playing for keeps, where the result may be win all or lose all, witnesses may well be partisan and disposed toward following any indication by counsel of the preferable line of testimony. The witness might not lie but obviously the effect of susceptibility to questions cannot be ignored. This would be a justification for the custom against permitting leading one's own witness.

Nevertheless, the existence of partisanship does not lead to the conclusion that leading questions necessarily induce distorted testimony. Rather our findings cast sufficient doubt on the soundness of the rule to suggest examination into the nature of partisanship and its relation to testimony. How do witnesses perceive their role? How is this conception affected by the rituals of the courtroom such as oaths and expressions of judicial authority? To what extent can a trier of fact discount whatever increase of suggestiveness is inherent in the use of leading questions?

When we compared the free reports of our witnesses with their answers under interrogation, we discovered a small though statistically significant trend for suspicious witnesses to give more testimony and more correct testimony than less suspicious witnesses. Possibly the feeling that the interrogator desired him to make mistakes encouraged the witness to meet the challenge in order to maintain his own self-image and sense of social power.[207]

---

[205] Zimbardo, *op. cit.*

[206] See Bem, *supra.* note 204.

[207] *See generally* N. Freyberg, *The Effect of Mistrust in Interpersonal Decision-Making on Hostility,* 1963 (unpublished doctoral dissertation in N.Y.U. Library) and see discussion ch. III, at p. 39, *supra.*

So we are left with the question: will hostility stimulate a partisan witness to recall better or merely encourage him to dissemble in order to win a point? Or both?

Lipton conducted a splendid experiment somewhat similar to ours.[208] The subjects were 40 male and 40 female undergraduate students. They were shown a film portraying a peaceful scene in a Los Angeles area park in which a man is suddenly shot and robbed. They were then interrogated in a number of ways. Lipton tried to avoid the facilitating effect of prior statements by using different witnesses in his unstructured and structured interrogations. Each witness was further interrogated by various types of questions: open-ended, leading and multiple choice. There was a week's delay in the interrogation of some witnesses and it was found that the delay had greater effect on the amount of recall than on the accuracy. There was no difference between written and oral testimony. Some questions were asked with a positive bias, some with a negative bias and some were neutral. There was no difference found in the amount of testimony in reply to positive and negative biases, but in both cases there was a significantly greater quantity than that in response to neutral questions.

Over all, he found that structured testimony was considerably less accurate than unstructured and was of much greater quantity. The explanation given is that when witnesses give unstructured testimony their cognitive state is under the least restraint and they are likely to give *only* testimony about which they are somewhat certain, with the result that accuracy is high and quantity low. It is not clear to what extent the salience of the items dealt with was considered in the structured conditions. Furthermore, as each witness was interrogated in several ways and different items of recall were involved in the several forms of interrogation, comparison with our results is difficult.

One extremely interesting finding by Lipton is that "female witnesses responded significantly more accurately to the questioning than did male witnesses... though the difference in quantity was insignificant." It would be good to have an analysis of the type of items covered by the questions. It may well be that certain kinds of questions elicit more precise recall from women

---

[208] *On the Psychology of Eye Witness Testimony,* J. APPLIED PSYCHOLOGY, 62, 90 (1977).

than from men and vice-versa because their experiences, expectations and, therefore, perceptions would differ. At any rate, Lipton suggests that additional research comparing testimony of men and women should be conducted as well as the effects of the sex of the interrogator.

It is well recognized that a prior interrogation or statement will have "a facilitating effect upon subsequent narrative recall."[209] Loftus, Altman and Geballe did an experiment testing the effects of such prior interrogation on subsequent recall.[210] A film was shown to the subjects which showed the disruption of a classroom by eight demonstrators. The subjects (witnesses) were then questioned. Half were asked in an "active" manner, *i.e.,* "Did you notice the militants *threatening* any of the students?" and "Did the professor *shout* something at the activists?" The other half were questioned in a more "passive" way, *i.e.,* "Did you notice the demonstrators *gesturing* at any students?" and "Did the professor *say* anything to the demonstrators?" (Italics added.)

A week later, without reviewing the film, they were asked a series of twenty questions about the event shown. The questions asked for a description of the incident as quiet or noisy, peaceful or violent, pacifistic or belligerent, sympathetic or antagonistic. "The results supported the hypothesis that the descriptions of witnesses to a complex incident can be influenced by the questions used to interrogate them about the incident. Specifically, the subjects in the present experiment who were interrogated with questions worded in an active, agressive manner reported that the incident they witnessed was noisier and more violent, that the perpetrators of the incident were more belligerent and that the recipients were more antagonistic" than those who had been initially interrogated in the more passive way. The conclusion of the researchers was that the data suggest strongly that *the first*

---

[209] Cady, *On the Psychology of Testimony,* AMERICAN J. PSYCHOLOGY, Vol. 35, 110 (1924); Whitely & McGeoch, *The Effect of One Form of Report upon Another,* AMERICAN J. PSYCHOLOGY, Vol. 38, 280 (1924); Snee & Lush, *Interaction of the Narrative and Interrogatory Methods of Obtaining Testimony,* J. PSYCHOLOGY, Vol. 11, 229 (1941); Lipton, *On the Psychology of Eye Witness Testimony,* J. APPLIED PSYCHOLOGY, 62, 90, 92 (1977). Of course it would be rare that a witness in litigation would not be questioned in advance by counsel, an investigator, the police or a prosecuting attorney.

[210] *Effects of Questioning upon A Witness' Later Recollections,* J. POLICE SCIENCE & ADMINISTRATION, Northwestern Univ. School of Law, 3 (1975).

investigator who interrogates the witness "can substantially color the way the witness sees and reports the incident." (Italics added.) It is suggested that a practical implication would be that the court give consideration to which side had the opportunity of initial interrogation of each witness. This would mean that a jury should be alerted to such an implication. See, again, McCarty on the preparation of witnesses.[211]

In another article [212] Loftus reports on an experiment in which a traffic accident was shown on a film. Afterwards the subjects were interrogated concerning the speed of the vehicle in one of two ways: (1) "About how fast were the cars going when they *smashed* into each other?" and (2) "About how fast were the cars going when they *hit* each other?" (Italics added.) The former question resulted in a much higher estimate of the speed of the cars.

A week later, without again reviewing the film, the subjects were asked a number of questions about the accident. The critical question asked was "Did you see any broken glass?" There was no broken glass in the picture. But as high speed accidents may suggest broken glass, it was anticipated that those witnesses asked the question containing the word "smashed" might more often state that they had seen broken glass than those who were asked the question without the word "smashed," *i.e.,* "hit." And this is what they found.

Testimony may not be affected by the atmosphere of interrogation but it may be affected by the kind of interrogation, the words used in interrogation, the sex of the witness and the witness's stress. We find, then, an array of variables affecting testimony and a mine to be explored further.

[211] See note, Chapt. I, p. 16.
[212] *Eye Witness,* PUGET SOUNDINGS (1975).

CHAPTER V

CONCERNING "THE COMMON SENSE JUDGMENT OF A GROUP OF LAYMEN" OR WHAT IS A FAIR JURY?

Influence of Public and Press on Fairness

In the Anglo-American judicial system the jury has gone through a number of forms. By the seventeenth century it was understood, in the words of Lord Coke, that a juror must be as "indifferent as he stands unsworn." In 1807 Chief Justice Marshall said, "The theory of the law is that a juror who has formed an opinion cannot be impartial." [213]

Although it is a crime to tamper with the jury, jurors are under constant pressure from newspapers, television, and radio, which may prejudge the case or at least the witnesses. From these sources, jurors may receive documents and testimony excluded by the judge. At a trial of Billy Sol Estes in Texas, his lawyers, during the impaneling of the jury, said that the only acceptable venireman was one of Latin-American origin who could neither read nor write, the assumption being that the others had already been exposed to too much prejudicial material in the press. The British are more realistic and prohibit such interference by the mass media. They have no first amendment right in conflict with a right to a fair trial.

The vital question was asked by Mr. Justice Frankfurter in a concurring opinion in *Irvin v. Dowd.* "How can fallible men and women reach a disinterested verdict based exclusively on what they heard in court when, before they entered the jury box, their minds were saturated by press and radio for months preceding by matter designed to establish the guilt of the accused?" [214]

In answer to this rhetorical question social scientists assure us that in such circumstances juries cannot close their minds to

---

[213] Quoted in *Irvin v. Dowd,* 366 U.S. 717, 722, 81 S.Ct. 1639, 1642 (1961). See also Holmes, J. in *Patterson v. Colorado,* 205 U.S. 454, 462, 27 S.Ct. 556, 558 (1907), "The theory of our system is that the conclusions to be reached in a case will be induced only by evidence and argument in open court, and not by any outside influence, whether of private talk or public print."

[214] *Op. cit.* U.S. 728, S.Ct. 729 and 730.

environmental pressures. They cannot be "impartial." They cannot be "indifferent." However, the courts are by no means consistent about what outside influences invalidate a judgment of guilt.

In *Frank v. Mangum,*[215] *habeas corpus* was denied after defendant's conviction for murder. The trial occurred in a courtroom "packed with spectators and surrounded by a crowd outside, all strongly hostile to the petitioner." The trial judge expressed the opinion to the defendant's counsel that there would be "probable danger of violence" to the counsel and the prisoner "in the event of an acquittal or disagreement" and suggested that it would be safer for them to be absent when the verdict was brought in. In a dissenting opinion, concurred in by Mr. Justice Hughes, Mr. Justice Holmes stated:

". . . Mob law does not become due process of law by securing the assent of a terrorized jury. We are not speaking of mere disorder, or mere irregularities in procedure, but of a case where the processes of justice are actually subverted."

". . . It is our duty to act . . . and to declare lynch law as little valid when practiced by a regularly drawn jury as when administered by one elected by a mob intent on death." [216]

Eight years later, Holmes wrote the majority opinion granting *habeas corpus* in a similar situation.[217] At that trial "The Court and neighborhood were thronged with an adverse crowd that threatened the most dangerous consequences to anyone interfering with the desired result." The trial lasted three-quarters of an hour and in five minutes the jury returned a verdict of guilty of murder.

It is not only mobs that can affect fair trial. The mass media may produce a situation in which a defendant cannot receive a fair trial before a jury contaminated by news reports.

A conflict occurs in many instances between freedom of the press to publish all it knows or hears or sees and a defendant's right to a fair trial by an impartial jury. It is a conflict between

---

[215] 237 U.S. 309, 35 S.Ct. 582 (1915).

[216] *Op. cit.* U.S. 347 and 350, S.Ct. 595 and 596. The death sentence was subsequently commuted by the governor to life imprisonment. Thereafter, Frank was seized by the mob and lynched and the governor was defeated for reelection.

[217] *Moore v. Dempsey,* 261 U.S. 86 and 89; 43 S.Ct. 265 and 266 (1923).

applications of the First and the Second and Fourteenth Amendments. Obviously certain kinds of publicity are prejudicial. For example, where the press reports items that are inadmissible in evidence, where comments are made by a trial judge on the guilt of the defendant, where there is public material never offered as evidence in court, where there is publication of confessions (forced or voluntary), where there is reference to prior convictions or allusions that are derogatory to the character of the defendant, where the defendant is reported to have refused to submit to a lie detector test and, finally, where guilt of the defendant is imputed by state officials.[218] However, the obvious prejudicial results of such publicity are not consistently accepted by the states as cause for reversal or even change of venue.

Inflammatory articles are deemed prejudicial but there is no clear test of what may be inflammatory. One criterion may be the extent of publicity or its frequency; another is the source. Adverse publicity that derives from a prosecutor, judge or the police is generally considered prejudicial. The public tends to give special credence to statements by such authorities. Extreme examples of this are TV confessions staged by the authorities and reenactments of a crime arranged by the police.

In especially notable (or notorious) cases it may take several years before the environment becomes sufficiently fumigated to enable a defendant to get a fair trial. Leon Jaworski, the special prosecutor of the Watergate cases, estimated that if President (ex-President) Nixon had been indicted it might have required a year, possibly longer, before a jury could be impannelled.[219] There had been articles in the press, the presentation live on television of the impeachment hearings before the House Judiciary Committee, a vote of impeachment and publication of the presidential tapes. Conditions necessary for a fair determination of the criminal charges against Nixon were estimated by others to necessitate an interval of several years.[220]

While the Supreme Court has in a number of instances overturned state court convictions that were obtained in an atmosphere "utterly corrupted by press coverage," this is not

---

[218] Dubnoff, *Pre-Trial Publicity and Due Process in Criminal Proceedings,* POLITICAL SCIENCE Q., 92, 97 (1977).

[219] Jaworski, THE RIGHT AND THE POWER 291 (1977).

[220] See also *Delaney v. U.S.,* 199 F.2d 107 (1952).

always the situation. In *Murphy v. Florida*,[221] the Supreme Court upheld a state conviction even though for a considerable time the press had given adverse information about the defendant, including his past criminal record. In a concurring opinion Chief Justice Burger underscored the court's differentiation between pre-trial "bizarre media coverage" in federal and state trials: "Although I would not hesitate to reverse petitioner's conviction in the exercise of our supervisory powers, were this a federal case, I agree with the Court that the circumstances of petitioner's trial did not rise to the level of a violation of the Due Process Clause of the Fourteenth Amendment." [222]

And state decisions have been contradictory. In one case Pennsylvania found reversible error, in part, because the crime had been restaged and this had been filmed and broadcast, which in itself was deemed a confession. In Illinois, on the other hand, where a mock trial was conducted, witnesses appearing on television identifying the defendant and containing excerpts from a confession, all published before the trial, the court regretted the practice but declined to reverse.[223]

As Dubnoff said:

". . . It is simply not reasonable that publication of a confession can inherently taint a federal trial but not have the same effect on a trial in many of the states. Surely, state jurors are not more immune to influence." [224]

Now, let us look at some empirical studies. Padawer-Singer and her associates experimented with jurors from an official jury pool in collaboration with members of the judiciary, a district attorney and members of the news media. All of the jurors read newspaper clippings that dealt with facts admissible in the trial. Half the jurors were selected with and half were selected without voir dire examinations. Half of each of these groups, in addition, "read newspaper clippings which also included information deemed

[221] 421 U.S. 794, 95 S.Ct. 2031 (19˝

[222] *Id.,* U.S. 803-04, S.Ct. 2038 (19ı5).

[223] See *Commonwealth v. Pierce,* 303 A.2d 209 (1973) and *People v. Torres,* 297 N.E.2d 142 (1973); also *Oliver v. State,* 250 So. 2d 888 (1971) and compare *State v. Hebard,* 184 N.W.2d 156 (1971).

[224] Dubnoff, *op. cit.* 108.

prejudicial to the defendant, namely an account of his criminal background and an alleged retracted confession. Thus, all the jurors were exposed to newspaper coverage of the alleged crime, but only half were exposed to prejudicial information." A tape that was based on the transcript of a real trial was played for the jurors, and after listening to the tape they deliberated and rendered their verdicts. They answered questionnaires and were interviewed. Their deliberations were taped with their knowledge and consent.

The data of the experiment showed:

"When jurors are selected randomly without voir dire examinations, 78.3 per cent of 'exposed' jurors as compared to [sic] 11.6 per cent of 'not exposed' jurors vote for guilty." [225]

These findings are supported by Kalven and Zeisel (The Chicago Jury Project) who found that jurors were affected by knowledge that defendants had a record.[226]

---

[225] Alice M. Padawer-Singer, et al., *Voir Dire By Two Lawyers: An Essential Safeguard*, JUDICATURE 57, 389 (1974).

[226] KALVEN and ZEISEL, THE AMERICAN JURY 389-90 (Little, Brown & Company 1966).

In the Chicago Jury Project two separate modes of inquiry were used. One involved interviewing actual jurors selected through the courts; the other involved simulation of jury panels selected by behavioral scientists. The latter was necessary because it was not permissible for the project to hear actual deliberations in the jury room.

The work with actual juries included having an observer present throughout the trial, interviewing each juror in depth after trial to compare the first-ballot and final verdict positions. Such inquiry found that in 71% of the cases the jury was not unanimous on the first ballot, and that in 36% of the cases the division was at least 8 to 4. The project found very few instances in which the minority view ultimately prevailed, that where the original minority was only one or two it was always overwhelmed, and that hung juries occurred only when there was a substantial minority, that is, where the dissenters found substantial support.

This can be explained by the fact that one who deviates from the group goal, in this case reaching a verdict, will feel more rejection by the other members of the group than where the deviation is irrelevant to the group's goal. Schachter, *Deviation, Rejection and Communication*, 46 J. ABNORMAL PSYCHOLOGY 190-207 (1951). See also Asch, *Studies of Independence and Conformity: A Minority of One Against an Unanimous Majority*, PSYCHOLOGICAL MONOGRAPHS, 70 (9, Whole No. 416) (1956).

The Jury Project was also interested in attitudes toward jury service both before and after participation. The major result here was "generally an affirmative response to jury service" but with major objections to the waste of time and the economic loss that such service entailed.

Similarly, other studies disclose that it was prejudicial to the defendant if there was pre-trial knowledge of his criminal record and confession.[227] Hoiberg and Stires distinguished between publicity that accentuated the horror or sensationalism of a crime and publicity "that links the defendant to the criminal act."[228] Perhaps sensationalism is what the Court had in mind when it spoke of inflammatory or "bizarre" media coverage.

Padawer-Singer et al. also concluded that a voir dire conducted by opposing lawyers reduced the effect of the prejudicial exposure and seemed "to insure the selection of the . . . most impartial jurors, jurors who will examine all sides of the trial." [229] How much of this effect is due to the elimination of prejudiced jurors through the voir dire and how much due to the statement of the issues by counsel is unclear.

When one considers the process of jury selection *one must wonder whether the purpose is to select a jury that is fair and*

The experimental Jury Project technique involved recordings of mock trials that were based on actual trials. The same tapes were played to different juries, or sometimes one element of the trial was changed to measure the impact of that element on the jury. The deliberations of these juries have been recorded, with the full knowledge of the participants. The jurors have also been interviewed before the completion of the trial. They were questioned before the deliberations began, and afterwards, and asked to describe their change of mind, if one occurred. Three moot cases have been developed thus far and played to over 50 moot juries. The project reports that jurors seem to get totally involved in their deliberations and give them full attention. Juries have hung, and have deliberated at great length. The three cases used deal with an automobile accident injury, an insanity defense comparing the effects of the *M'Naghten* and *Durham* rules, and a products liability suit. This project has also done some work on comparing the verdicts that jurors reach with those of judges in the same case, and have found that the two correlate more closely than expected. The principal cause of divergence was differing values. See Kalven and Zeisel, THE AMERICAN JURY (1966).

[227] Siebert, *Trial Judges' Opinions and Prejudicial Publicity* in FREE PRESS AND FAIR TRIAL 1-35 (Bush ed. 1970); Tans & Chaffee. *Pretrial Publicity and Juror Prejudice,* JOURNALISM Q. 43:647-54 (1966).

[228] Hoiberg & Stires, *The Effect of Several Types of Pretrial Publicity on the Guilt Attributions of Simulated Jurors,* J. OF APPLIED SOCIAL PSYCHOLOGY, 3, 267-275 (1973), cited by Wrightsman, *The American Trial Jury on Trial: Empirical Evidence and Procedural Modifications,* JOURNAL OF SOCIAL ISSUES, 34, 4 (1978).

[229] *Op. cit.* 389. "1. When jurors are selected randomly without voir dire examinations, 78.3 per cent of 'exposed' jurors as compared to [sic] 11.6 per cent of 'not exposed' jurors vote for guilty.

"2. When jurors are selected with voir dire examinations, 60 per cent of exposed jurors as compared to [sic] 50 per cent of 'not exposed' jurors vote for guilty."

impartial or one that is favorable to a party.[230] Whatever the theory lawyers would try to have a jury empanelled favorable to their side of the case. Most lawyers have their own rule of thumb about jury selection but most would question the certainty of achieving their end. Unfavorable jurors might be eliminated by a voir dire but even this process can never with certainty provide data that any particular juror would be unfavorable.[231]

When the courts have recognized impropriety of verdicts influenced by happenings beyond the courtroom or by matter properly not evidentiary, they have moral justification and support from scientific research. What can be said, however, of courts that fail to see or value the effects of out-of-court or inadmissible happenings on the fairness of a trial? And why is it justice and fair trial to rule against such influences on a jury in a federal court and not in a state court? Defendants in such cases would appear to be the victims of federalism. It would seem that a notorious criminal would be wise to include in his malice aforethought commission of a crime triable in a federal rather than a state court.

How Many Equals Fair?

A defendant in a criminal case and the parties in a civil case are entitled to an independent jury that has not prejudged the case but not to a jury of any particular size. Nor need the jury be unanimous. In a series of decisions the Supreme Court has held that there is no constitutional right to a jury of twelve. Six person juries have been consistently upheld in recent years.[232] In all these cases the opinions of the court use as authorities some empirical studies concerning the validity of the verdicts of juries smaller than twelve.

Saks has analyzed the empirical studies used in *Williams* and *Colgrove* and come to the conclusion "On the basis of non-studies and misread studies, the Supreme Court decided *Williams.* On the basis of the flawed studies conducted after *Williams,* the same conclusion was reinforced in *Colgrove.* And armed with these

---

[230] Wrightsman, *supra.*

[231] Broeder, *Voir Dire Examinations: An Empirical Study,* S. CAL. L. REV., 38, 503-28 (1965).

[232] *Williams v. Florida,* 399 U.S. 78, 90 S.Ct. 1893 (1970); *Colgrove v. Battin,* 413 U.S. 149, 93 S.Ct. 2448 (1973); *Ballew v. Georgia,* 435 U.S. 223, 98 S.Ct. 1029 (1978).

studies and the Court's opinions, rapidly increasing numbers of federal district courts have reduced the size of civil juries to six, Congress has considered legislation requiring the use of six-member juries in civil trial juries throughout the federal court system . . . and state court systems around the nation have reduced or are considering reduction of the size of juries. . . ." [233] While he found little difference in the judgments of twelve person and six person juries in civil cases, Saks suggests that in making a determination of which is better one must select among the values: "large juries because they provide for the representation of a wider cross-section of the community" or small juries "because they induce a better proportional recall of arguments" although not necessarily as many items of evidence.[234]

He found juries of twelve to be preferable to juries of six in that they produced longer deliberations, more communications, better community representation and also possibly greater verdict consistency, which he called reliability. On the other hand, the small jury advantages were more participation per juror, communication more evenly shared and better proportional recall of arguments and also possibly fewer convictions.

In *Ballew* the Court (and, it might be read, rather half-heartedly) confirmed its previous judgments validating six person juries but ruled that juries of five were inadequate.[235]

The opinion stated that research suggests that as juries become smaller deliberations in criminal cases vary to the detriment of the defense and also, among other things, as the size of the jury decreases there are not only problems for jury-decision-making "but also for the representation of minority groups in the community."

Saks [236] found in his experiments that twelve person juries provided "substantially more representative cross-section of the community" than did six person juries.

---

[233] Saks, JURY VERDICTS 38-55, 55 (1977). Cited a number of times by Mr. Justice Blackmun in *Ballew*. And see Wrightsman, *supra*, when research relied on by the Court was found to be technically unreliable.

[234] *Op. cit.* 106-07.

[235] Mr. Justice Blackmun pointed out that post-*Williams* studies "raise significant doubts about the consistency and reliability of the decisions of smaller juries."

[236] *Op. cit.* 91 et seq.

Similarly, Padawer-Singer and Barton [237] concluded the larger jury to be more representative of a cross-section of population than smaller juries, using census figures of the jurisdiction for comparison. Thus, there were blacks on 59% of the six member juries and on 78% of the twelve member juries. Jurors who answered "other" rather than black or white were represented in only 3% of the twelve member juries and on none of the six member juries. Women were on 30% of the six member juries compared with 57% of the twelve member juries. Two or more women were on only 2% of the six member juries but 22% of the twelve member juries. Similarly, the larger juries had a wider distribution of members of various age groups and vocational levels. "In the 6-member juries the socio-economic ratings tended to be concentrated in the middle ranges, while in the 12-member juries the range distribution tends to be more equally distributed to the lower and higher categories." [238] And again [239] "In the categories of Sex, Age, and Education any deviance from the voter registration population may be accounted for by built-in biases in the juror selection process. But in terms of population representativeness: Race, Occupational data, and Socio-Economic Status; the 6-member jury tends to be less heterogeneous than the 12-member jury."

They also state that the court in *Williams* offered no real evidence to support its assertion that although in theory the number of viewpoints on a jury ought to increase as the size of the jury increases "in practice the difference between the 12-man jury and the 6-man jury in terms of the cross-section of the community represented seems likely to be negligible."

Padawer-Singer and Barton question the court's contention that the jury's reliability as a fact-finder "hardly seems likely to be a function of size." [240]

These findings from empirical data suggest that the six person jury denies a party "meaningful community participation." This contrasts with the established norm that juries, as instruments of public justice, be bodies truly representative of the community.[241]

---

[237] Interim Report: *Experimental Study of Decision-Making in the 12- Versus 6-Man Jury Under Unanimous Versus Non-Unanimous Decisions,* by Padawer-Singer, Col. Univ., ch. XIV, 7-8 (1975).

[238] *Op. cit.,* ch. XIV, 9.

[239] *Op. cit.,* ch. XIV, 10.

[240] *Op. cit.,* ch. IX, 6.

[241] *Smith v. Texas,* 311 U.S. 128, 130, 61 S.Ct. 164, 165 (1940).

An important consideration in size of jury has been its representativeness. Juries have been held to be defective when women were excluded,[242] when blacks were excluded [243] and "all persons who worked for a daily wage had been deliberately and intentionally excluded from the jury list." [244] The studies indicate that the courts cannot have representative juries, juries representative of a broad cut of the population, if they accept 6-member juries. Further research is indicated concerning the propriety of 8- or 10-member juries.

However in *Apodaca* [245] it was held that although juries had to be representative of the community, every jury did not have to have a representative of every section or community. All that is forbidden is systematic exclusion of identifiable segments of the community. Thus a defendant could not challenge a jury because members of his race were not on it. It would be necessary to prove a systematic exclusion.

In *Williams* [246] it was pointed out that in capital cases no state has permitted juries of less than twelve "a fact that suggests implicit recognition of the value of the larger body as a means of legitimizing society's decision to impose the death penalty." If we concede a special value to a jury of twelve where a defendant's life is concerned, may not the possibility of a long term of imprisonment justify similar considerations?

The Supreme Court has also upheld verdicts by juries that are less than unanimous. In *Apodaca* [247] a verdict of ten out of twelve was held constitutionally sufficient, and in *Johnson v. Louisiana* [248] a verdict of nine out of twelve was supported. On this point Saks found that dissenters are not ignored by twelve person juries and that even when a verdict had been reached in twelve member quorum juries, the discussion continued.[249] This would mean that dissenters were not ignored and the majority still wanted to be reinforced by their agreement.

---

[242] *Ballard v. U.S.,* 329 U.S. 187, 67 S.Ct. 261 (1946).

[243] *Norris v. Alabama,* 294 U.S. 587, 55 S.Ct. 579 (1935) (the famous *Scottsboro* case); and *Strauder v. West Virginia,* 100 U.S. 303 (1880).

[244] *Thiel v. Southern Pacific Company,* 328 U.S. 217, 66 S.Ct. 984 (1946).

[245] *Apodaca v. Oregon,* 406 U.S. 404, 92 S.Ct. 1628 (1972).

[246] *Op. cit.* U.S. 103, S.Ct. 1907.

[247] *Op. cit.* U.S. 404, S.Ct. 1628.

[248] 406 U.S. 356, 92 S.Ct. 1635 and 1650, 1651 (1972).

[249] *Op. cit.* 93.

Reduction in the number of jurors and the removal of the requirement of unanimity remind us of the warning by Mr. Justice Black of the "gradual process of judicial erosion which ... has slowly worn away a major portion of the essential guarantee of the Seventh Amendment." [250] "Today, the erosion process reaches bedrock," Mr. Justice Marshall concluded in his dissenting opinion in *Williams.*

As Kalven and Zeisel found,[251] when juries and judges reach different conclusions on the identical evidence, it is because the jury "gives recognition to values which fall outside the official rules." Furthermore, in the determination of issues of fact a jury more than a judge tends to give weight "to the norm that there should be no conviction without proof beyond a reasonable doubt. And there is every indication that the jury follows the evidence and understands the case."

Our values are derived from our experiences. "When a person has an experience, he reduces it to a series of symbolic representations of that experience." [252] This becomes "symbolic memory" of events and feelings associated with them, that become coded and thus consciously or unconsciously affect the evaluation of later happenings and perception of them. This is illustrated by a finding by *Simon* in an experimental jury trial concerned with determining mental illness. "Indeed, if we were asked to name the one factor that was most influential in determining a juror's verdict, the extent to which the defendant resembled or failed to resemble someone whom the juror knew to be mentally ill would rank extremely high." [253]

In a trial in which one Herrin was accused of murder of a former girlfriend, and the defense was that the act was committed under great stress, after four days of deliberation the jury returned a verdict of manslaughter. Four jurors were interviewed after the verdict. "They described how they had confided in one another about their own emotional crises and how this had had some bearing on their view of the case." [254]

---

[250] *Galloway v. U.S.,* 319 U.S. 372, 397, 63 S.Ct. 1077, 1090 (1943) dissenting opinion.

[251] *Op. cit.* 494-95.

[252] Watson, PSYCHIATRY FOR LAWYERS, 62-63 (1968).

[253] Simon, THE JURY AND THE DEFENSE OF INSANITY 154 (1967).

[254] New York Times, June 22, 1978.

Experience of public opinion respecting the particular offense (criminal or civil), and sometimes a juror's own sense of but for the grace of God there sit I, are encoded in his value system. "The important point is that correct attribution, whether to the stable or to the vacillating conditions underlying an event, always serves to build up and support the constancy of our picture of the world." [255]

A jury may reject the application of laws that it considers unjust for local or more general reasons, such as sumptuary laws and poaching of alligators in the Everglades. In Minnesota a helicopter was spraying herbicide on a forest near a farm of one Seaver. Seaver claimed that this chemical caused his family to suffer headaches, nausea, dizziness and diarrhea. So he took a shot at the helicopter. The jury acquitted him of all charges, ruling that he was merely acting in defense of his home and property.[256]

"Some village Hampton that, with dauntless breast
The little tyrant of his fields withstood." [257]

Sometimes juries have rejected what they considered political persecution, as in seditious libel. Frequently, too, jurors have been suspicious of the catch-net of conspiracy indictments. And sometimes a jury's sense of what the law ought to be is law in another jurisdiction.[258]

To some degree our values are wishful thinking. As Cook pointed out, "One way of looking at values is that they describe conditions which their holders desire in some degree to exist." [259] This will account for differences between juries and judges, among juries, at different times and in different locales.

But values are also derived from conditions that do exist.

---

[255] HEIDER, THE PSYCHOLOGY OF INTERPERSONAL RELATIONS 92 (1958).

[256] Anderson, *Washington Merry-Go-Round,* Scottsdale Daily Progress, July 17, 1978.

[257] Gray, *Elegy Written in a Country Churchyard,* in THE HOME BOOK OF VERSE, 3304-06 (Stevenson ed. 1912).

[258] KALVEN & ZEISEL, *op. cit.* 497.

[259] Cook, *Motives in a Conceptual Analysis of Attitude Behavior,* in NEBRASKA SYMPOSIUM ON MOTIVATION, Lincoln: Univ. of Nebraska Press, 179-231 (ARNOLD & LEVINE eds. 1969).

Socio-economic classes and subcultures may differ critically in their values.[260] Fair and right for one may appear discriminatory and wrong to another. This makes clear the importance of giving defendants an opportunity to have as jurors people of different income levels and of different subcultures.

There is an old quatrain, from the time when the British landlords enclosed the village commons for their own use, illustrative of such conflicting values, that goes like this:

> "The law locks up both
> Man and woman
> Who steals the goose
> From off the Common
> But turns the greater
> Felon loose
> Who steals the Common
> From the goose."

Aristocracies and middle classes have historically required all members of society to accept their values through the instrumentality of laws. These do not commonly recognize lower class values or those peculiar to subcultures in the population. Poverty has its own "unacceptable" values. We find an expression of this by Mr. Doolittle, Eliza's father, in *Pygmalion:*[261]

> "I ask you, what am I? I'm one of the undeserving poor: thats what I am. Think of what that means to a man. It means that he's up agen middle class morality all the time.... What is middle class morality? Just an excuse for never giving me anything."

This difference in values (and of perceptions, too) is a fundamental *raison d'etre* for the jury system which makes available a buffer between a common sense view of the legitimacy and propriety of a claim and often vindictive prosecutors or judges — or powerful interests. For throughout history there have been many judges who acquire (or begin with) a prosecutorial mind-set. There have always been some judges of the nature of Lord Jeffries

---

[260] MARSHALL, INTENTION IN LAW AND SOCIETY ch. II (1968).
[261] SHAW, PYGMALION, Penguin Books, Act II, 48-49 (1951).

of the Bloody Assizes. And many a judge is a graduate prosecuting attorney. There is no opportunity for a voir dire of judges.[262]

The reduction in the size of juries and the authorization of less than unanimous verdicts are frequently justified by the expectations of more convictions in less time. This accords with the mood of our time for stricter law enforcement. But there is no empirical evidence that there is much economy in trial time, or time of jury deliberation. A greater proportion of convictions where quorum verdicts are permitted rather than a required unanimity, appears to be due to fewer hung juries.[263]

Urge to Convict and Effects of Authority

There is in human nature an urge to convict.

"Our righteous indignation against wrongdoers is more often than we consciously realize an expression of our own strong but repressed aggressive impulses. The urge to punish in others the misconduct we repress in ourselves is probably the main obstacle to the adoption of a rational penal code." [264]

Moreover, a large proportion of us, though trained not to hurt others intentionally, will practice cruelty when legitimatized by authority. This was most dramatically illustrated by the German people's acceptance of the viciousness of the Nazi regime.

An experiment by Milgram [265] also indicates this. Collaborators were asked questions by subjects and when the wrong answer was given subjects, on instructions of the experimenter, gave the collaborators "electric shocks," increasing in severity as the experiment proceeded. Actually no shock was given but the collaborators acted with increasing evidences of suffering as the shocks increased, shouting as though in pain. "In this situation a subject is instructed to perform acts that are in some sense incompatible with his normal standards of behavior. In the face of

---

[262] A motion that a judge disqualify himself for prejudice is not often granted and, in any event, is not comparable with a voir dire.

[263] "To the extent that hung juries have the same effect as acquittals on the defendant's freedom, greater ease in reaching a verdict means less protection for the defendant." SAKS, *op. cit.* 102.

[264] WEIHOFEN, THE URGE TO PUNISH 13 (1956), quoted in SIMON, *op. cit.* 170.

[265] Milgram, *Liberating Effects of Group Pressure,* J. PERSONALITY & SOCIAL PSYCHOLOGY, 127-34 (1965).

the vehement protest of an innocent individual, many subjects refused to carry out the experimenter's orders to continue the shock procedure. . . . Fourteen of the 40 subjects withdrew from the experiment at some point before the completion of the command series." [266] But 26 continued to the end. Although they did not wish to hurt the victim they felt obligated to follow orders.

In a second experiment two additional confederates sat with the subject. The latter applied the electric shocks on instructions from the experimenter. After "150-volts" had been administered one of the confederates refused to go along further. After "210-volts" had been administered the second confederate indicated his distress and refused to continue. At this point 36 of 40 subjects refused to go forward and defied the experimenter as compared with 14 in experiment 1.

In another study [267] Milgram varied the task of the two confederates. This time they called for increasingly more powerful shocks. The subject again had control of the level of shock which he could hold down or increase. In thirty trials the shock levels were increased in accordance with the pressure of the confederates. (In reality there was no shock administered but again the "victim" behaved as though reacting to increased shock.) "The substantive contribution of the present study," Milgram said, "lies in the demonstration that group influence can shape behavior in a domain that might have been thought highly resistant to such effects. Subjects are induced by the group to inflict pain on another person at a level that goes well beyond levels chosen in the absence of social pressure.[268]

The indication is that group influence, as well as authority, definitely affects behavior.

In his now classic experiment, Sherif compared the relationship of the perception of people who first made observations singly and then in groups. Of those who made their first observations in groups and later singly, he concluded:

"There is a tendency to converge toward a common norm and to experience the situation as regulated and ordered by

---

[266] Op. cit. 128.
[267] Milgram, Group Pressure and Action Against a Person, J. ABNORMAL AND SOCIAL PSYCHOLOGY, 69, 137-43 (1964).
[268] Op. cit. 141.

this norm. The group must be right. 'There's safety in numbers.' . . . Once the common norm is established, later the separate individuals keep on perceiving it in terms of the frame of reference which was once the norm of the group." [269]

It would seem from Milgram's experiments that a minority of more than one on a jury, that is a minority with support, could resist majority pressure, if the minority believes that a verdict of guilty would be hurtful. Other research has shown that the tendency of jurors is to favor plaintiffs or prosecution.

If conviction is the principal aim there are, of course, surer and speedier ways to obtain this than by adversary trial by jury. The Soviet system of deciding political judgments in advance and permitting no defense, and Idi Amin's method in Uganda of placing the accused promptly before a firing squad are more effective means of prosecution — in every sense indefensible.

If there be limits to the smallness of a fair jury there are also limits to its enlargement as indicated by the case of Condorcet, the eighteenth century French philosopher. He proposed that errors in judgment might be minimized, on the mathematical theory of probability, if the size of a tribunal be so increased as to neutralize extremes of prejudice. Unfortunately, a large revolutionary tribunal holding a uniformly extreme view remanded him to the guillotine.

The line between effective law enforcement and the protection of the rights of the accused, may sometimes appear obscure. Nevertheless, the ethical principle of Anglo-American law that it is better for ten guilty to go free than to convict one innocent man or woman must be given high priority if we are to remain a free people. And, of course, if an innocent is convicted a guilty will go free.

The Shadow of Appellate Courts

A frequent question is what is an issue of fact to be submitted to a jury? In other words, what question of "fact" is to be submitted to "the common sense judgment of a group of laymen" and what is to be withheld in the preserve of judicial competence? "Here is the rub, for 'fact' is a highly variable concept that would

---

[269] SHERIF, THE PSYCHOLOGY OF SOCIAL NORMS 95-111 (1936).

not submit to stable definition but takes its meaning from its context." [270] And that context surely includes the validity of perception and recall and the credibility of the source of the evidence. To determine what is a question of fact for a jury or a fact not to be entrusted to a jury but decided by a judge is a matter of law. Sometimes law and fact become as entwined as though a double helix.

Frequently the trial court is not the final institution for finding fact, the truth of the occurrences, with which a litigation is concerned. Appeals are so readily available that effectively a "remote control" is given to the appellate courts. As Dean Green points out, however accurate and conscientious a record on appeal may be, it

> ". . . has little resemblance to jury trial as it had developed in Anglo-American judicial history. . . . Moreover, the trial may be recorded with the utmost fidelity, but many of its overtones and undertones do not find their way in the record. In the trial court the case is pulsing with life: by the time it reaches the appellate court, much of its life has leaked out or evaporated. Again, the objectives of the two courts are somewhat different. In the trial court the emphasis is on justice as between the parties; in the appellate court it is on keeping the lines of the law straight and systematic for justice in general." [271]

In this sense appellate courts are not merely adjudicators but also law-makers. The Common Law is probably the greatest contribution by judges in their "legislative" capacity that any courts have made. Judges at all levels, taking their tasks seriously, write opinions which, if not to endure for eternity, at least they hope will have enduring effects. (It is perhaps similar to the Godlike stance of editorial writers.) Juries, on the other hand, act in and for the present.

So now what do we have: witnesses whose perception and recall are imperfect (even when they testify in good faith),[272] giving

---

[270] Green, *The Submission of Issues in Negligence Cases*, MIAMI L. REV., XVIII, No. 1 (1963).

[271] Green, *Jury Trial and Mr. Justice Black*, YALE L.J., Vol. LXV, No. 4, (1965).

[272] In the discussion of the imperfections of perception and recall it has been here assumed that the testimony, no matter how inaccurate, was in good faith. But see McCabe, p. 6 *supra*.

evidence to a judge and jurors who may perceive and recall just as imperfectly as witnesses do, and a record on appeal to judges who neither see nor hear the evidence but read about it, and who are less concerned with the realities of the specific case before them than with what their opinions (their declarations of what the law is) may mean to future courts and litigants.[273] In this atmosphere "the common sense judgment of a group of laymen" becomes clouded.

---

[273] And so one arrives at a situation in which we get long majority opinions (or opinions of the court), long dissenting opinions, concurring opinions, additional dissenting opinions as if each judge must make clear to posterity every little disagreement with his brothers on the bench. Perhaps the egocentric culture of our day has infected the whole of American society including the Supreme Court.

CHAPTER VI

IN THE COURTROOM

Advocacy as a Change Process

Thus far we have been considering principally perception, recollection, and articulation as they affect a witness to a happening or event; and also some psychological aspects of mass media effects on juries and of the composition of juries. We have discussed the relativity of reality in such transactions and the "As If" assumption of some of the rules of evidence. Now we shall focus on the psychological transactions and inter-relationships of advocacy and fact-finding, the attorneys and the judge and jury.

The lawyer's concern with reality is not only with fact but also effect. He must evaluate evidence in terms of how it will appear to the judge and jury. Normally in contract negotiation or in litigation there is a play for position. That is part of the game. But the successful lawyer, however just he may deem his cause or with whatever assurance he may present it, cannot afford to indulge in psychological *denial* of *facts,* disagreeable, incongruent facts, which may be presented by his opponent. He cannot afford to close his mind to the *interpretations* his opponent might offer in the course of his advocacy.

A lawyer or negotiator must also constantly be aware of how *his* reality will appear not only to his opponent but to such neutrals as the judge and jury.

"A good prosecutor is generally one who has had to destroy a prosecutor's case from the defendant's side of the table. A prosecution witness can shine before a Grand Jury, where there is no cross examination, then completely fall apart when subjected to a defense attorney's questioning." [273a]

This is a different aspect of the problem of reality from that which is described by the testimony. The appearance of a piece of evidence to the judge and jury is a product of their expectations, experiences, belief systems, and sympathies, which make reality for them. Within the "As If" system of the law, the ultimate test

---

[273a] JAWORSKI, THE RIGHT AND THE POWER, Pocket, 17 (1977).

of reality to the lawyer is: will a witness or a piece of evidence succeed in moving the triers of fact to a response favorable to his case? Consequently, the manner in which evidence is presented may be to the trial counsel as important as the facts themselves. This is at least tacitly recognized in Great Britain, where the solicitor gathers the facts and the barrister presents them. It is increasingly common in this country, too, for special trial counsel to be retained.

The Change Process

The lawyer trying a case has the task of bringing about *change*. He must bring the attitude of judge and jury from neutrality or hostility to supportiveness. One effective way to bring about change is to involve the person or persons to be changed in the process of planning and installing the change.[274] It is scarcely feasible for judge and jury to be involved in such a self-changing process — at least within the law and our prevailing ethical principles. They can, however, be involved emotionally by stimulation in them of a tension, a need, a motive to change their attitudes to favorable ones. Consequently, theories of change become relevant.

When we are in conflict over some contradiction, some dissonant concepts, some ambivalence or imbalance of feeling, as in the case of conflicting evidence, we try to resolve it. We may attempt to eliminate conflict by ceasing to think about it, that is, we try to deny that the conflicting evidence exists. Counsel may attempt to get the jury to forget about an item of evidence by ignoring it or belittling it so that it appears irrelevant, unworthy of consideration or contradictory to other more credible evidence. If we feel that a piece of evidence really has little or no value, then we are relieved of whatever conflict it has caused.

Usually, however, counsel will attempt resolution by differentiation. For example, fifty miles an hour may have been the lawful speed limit but in this case the defendant was passing a truck and it was negligence not to have a clear view before making

---

[274] Coch & French, Jr., *Overcoming Resistance to Change,* 1 HUMAN RELATIONS 512-32 (1948).

the attempt. This was, then, a different situation than one in which fifty miles an hour would be legitimate, reasonable. The attorney does the same thing in arguing the law. The case of *A v. B* is irrelevant, he points out, because although in that case the facts *X* and *F* were present, here fact *Z* makes the case different. "So with the growth of law. The judge stretches a point here in response to a moral urge, or makes a new application of a precedent there. Before long a new tradition has arisen. . . . The moral norm and the jural have been brought together, and are one." [275] Differentiation is our common response to conflict pressures and therefore is an easy technique for the attorney and an acceptable one to court and jury.

This process of differentiation may not merely resolve a conflict, remove a block to the acceptance by the jury of counsel's case, it may at times change their attitude. For example, if it can be made to appear that the plaintiff was not just reckless in running to the middle of the highway but was trying to save a dog, the attitude of the jury may be changed from a negative to a positive one: the plaintiff was a hero.

Of course, the most effective way to change attitudes, to reduce dissonance or ambivalence, is to bring added social support to reinforce acceptance of the desired change or resolution. The degree of social support that a concept yields is related to the source of the concept. If we like or admire someone we tend to accept his ideas; and we reject them if we dislike or despise him. To a lesser extent, disliked ideas may reduce the lustre of an otherwise admired source and make him unacceptable, and vice versa.[276] In social research itself the acceptability of the experimenter appears to be a variable, the more admired experimenter seemingly being able to effect greater change in behavior.[277]

---

[275] CARDOZO, THE PARADOXES OF LEGAL SCIENCE 43 (1928), referring to VAIHINGER, DIE PHILOSOPHIE DES ALS OB [THE PHILOSOPHY OF THE "AS IF"] (Ogden transl. 1935).

[276] Brown, *Models of Attitude Change,* in BROWN, GALANTIER, HESS & MANDLER, NEW DIRECTIONS IN PSYCHOLOGY 1, 38 (Barron ed. 1962). The application of these models of attitude change, discussed by Brown, to the process of the law would appear to be a worthwhile area for research.

[277] *Id.* at 39, and see KALVEN & ZEISEL, *op. cit.* 385.

Counsel may be so acceptable to the jury that his words alone can give to a juryman the support necessary to reduce his conflict and change his attitude. But usually support in resolving conflict within the triers of fact is provided by presenting the evidence in such a way that doubtful testimony is reinforced by a succession of corroborating witnesses, examples from common experience, or, perhaps, documents and photographs.

Counsel wants to be accepted by judge and jury. He wants to win their support as a means to winning their judgment or verdict in his favor. Styles in the conduct of a case may differ and one attorney will be more sensitive to feedback from his interaction with judge and jury than another. Some, poor souls, can never appear as other than pettifoggers. By gaining acceptance from judge and jury, counsel not only gains their support but is in a position to support them in some attitude favorable to his case.

Having established his own acceptability, perhaps in the course of doing so, he then must build up his client and witnesses and if possible reduce the acceptability of the opposing parties and witnesses, so that in the scale of social acceptance his side will generate greater acceptance than the other. We could put this in another way: If a lawyer can achieve greater balance for his side of the case, then this will be supportive of jury and judge who render a verdict or judgment in his favor. They need support from him in return for meeting his need for their support. This support he provides them when he can make his case appear more reasonable to them, more consonant with their values and personal experiences, than his opponent's.

Values arise from expectations and so there is the tendency to accept what is expected of a situation. It is this that makes evidence credible, meeting the values of norms of judge and jury because it satisfies their expectations; or conversely it meets their expectations because it satisfies their values or norms. To make behavior appear normal, even the absurd reasonable, is an accepted problem of advocacy.

A trial lawyer is probably most successful if he introduces the contradictions, inaccuracies, or falsifications of the opposing witnesses, or the weakness of his opponent's interpretation, after he has established a supportive relationship between himself and the jury. In his advocacy the lawyer is not unlike the saleman who only after he "has established himself as a man of good taste . . .

can venture some esteem capital by speaking out for a sofa whose costliness renders it mildly negative for the customer and hope to draw that sofa sufficiently high on the value scale to bring it across the purchase threshold." [278]

This is well understood by trial lawyers. The good will, the acceptance earned by counsel is an investment in his cause. It makes possible a positive identification of himself with his client. For example, Gair says:

> "We must make full use of the psychological principle of identification: identification in the eyes of the jury between you and your client, and identification of the jury with what has befallen your client." [279]

It is often believed that such psychological approaches are not important in presenting cases to judges. Perhaps not. It would be interesting to find empirical evidence as to this belief. In any event, experienced trial lawyers do not believe that judges are immune from similar pressures and inter-relationships.[280] Nizer, speaking of a judge in a case, says:

> "No doubt he was trying to be ... impartial, but judges, like the rest of us, are affected by motivations so deep that they are hidden from their own awareness.... It was up to me to cast ... doubt in his mind as well as in the jury's collective mind."

He also suggests that when a judge reserves decision on a motion to dismiss at the end of the plaintiff's case, he has "a psychological involvement in a defendant's verdict." [281]

Psychological Transactions in the Trial

The jury, by being allowed to operate within the courtroom, becomes an arm of the court, nominally bound by the rules of law. However, in its operation, the jury is actually an expression of

---

[278] Brown, *op. cit. supra* note 276, at 37.

[279] Gair, *The Psychology of Litigation,* 20, No. 2 N.Y. COUNTY LAW. A.B. BULL. 44-49, at 48 (1962).

[280] STRYKER, THE ART OF ADVOCACY 32-34 (1954).

[281] NIZER, MY LIFE IN COURT 352 (1961).

public opinion. The court expresses the power of the state, the jury the feeling of a group of private individuals on a controversial issue. It would seem that the courts allow the jury to be a buffer between the law and the public. " 'It saves judges from the responsibility — which to many men would appear intolerably heavy and painful — of deciding simply on their own opinion upon the guilt or innocence of the prisoner.' It saved the judges of the middle ages not only from this moral responsibility, but also from enmities and feuds. Likewise it saved them from that as yet unattempted task, a critical dissection of testimony." [282]

Part of the great disparity between the jury and the law as vehicles of that elusive goal "justice" is that the laws that govern jury trials do not take cognizance of what we now know about many aspects of human behavior. The assumptions basic to a jury trial may be "illusory," as Judge Jerome Frank called them. This is particularly true in automobile personal injury cases where the evidence deals essentially with matters of common experience and individual perception.

In most automobile accident cases there are several eyewitnesses whose testimony will be in conflict on crucial points.[283] Judge or jury is asked to decide which side's witnesses

---

[282] 2 POLLOCK & MAITLAND, THE HISTORY OF ENGLISH LAW 627 (2d ed. 1898). It has been suggested by Leifer that "The use of a 'scientific expert' to aid in the determination of responsibility eases the burden of the court by giving the impression that the determination rests on a scientifically determined fact rather than on an ambiguous matter of semantics. It thus disguises and distracts us from the fact that the courts have to justify life and death decisions on the basis of arbitrary and ambiguous criteria and provides what appears to be a scientific justification for the court's decision." Leifer, *The Psychiatrist and Tests of Criminal Responsibility* 19, 11 AMERICAN PSYCHOLOGIST 827 (1964).

[283] Examples of conflicting perceptions of witnesses which must be resolved are to be found in the 1964 *Warren Commission Report* 115, 133, 169, which analyzed the evidence concerning the assassination of President Kennedy and the murder of Patrolman Tippitt. Most of the witnesses at the scene claimed to have heard three shots. But there were some who testified hearing four and "perhaps as many as five or six shots." "Soon after the three empty cartridges were found, officials at the scene decided that three shots were fired, and that conclusion was widely circulated by the press. The eyewitness testimony may be subconsciously colored by the extensive publicity given the conclusion that three shots were fired." (*Id.* at 110-11.)

A majority of the eyewitnesses said that the three shots were not evenly spaced, most recalling the second and third shots bunched together, but there were others

present the more probably accurate account of the incident. They must determine whether the party having the burden of proof has achieved a preponderance of evidence. This involves a value judgment and, however well defined by the courts, it remains largely subjective. *One man's preponderance is another's failure of proof.* And there are jurisdictions in which in a case involving persons of different races it requires a preponderant preponderance for one to win and pigmentation for the other.

"Preponderance" of the evidence is a general feeling. There is no objective criterion for determining it. From a feeling about the existence of preponderance, judge or jury has to make a specific finding within the specific definition of fault liability as to whether, for example, the defendant's action was negligent and led solely and directly to the injury, an abrupt transition from art to mathematics, a process of weighing and evaluating. In view of the fact that a trial rarely can produce perceptions that are true to objective reality, and can never be complete, a court decides a case on an estimate of probability, which is an element of its expectation.[284] The jury "accepts one version as against another because it accords with its own standard of experience. The judge, when he is faced with conflicting testimony, decides on the basis of probability. We talk of the credibility of witnesses, but what we

---

who thought that the first and second were. One well-placed witness recalled that the President was hit in the head by the last shot. Another, that there was a shot after the President was struck in the head. Two witnesses who testified to the bag in which Oswald was supposed to have carried the rifle estimated the size of the bag to be some six or seven inches shorter than the largest component of the rifle, and some ten inches shorter than the bag actually found. (*Id.* at 111 et seq., 133.)

Each of two sisters who positively identified Oswald in the line-up, whispering their identification to a detective, testified that she was the first one to make the identification. It would appear that an ego need of each prompted a claim to first place, and for one of them distorted reality. (*Id.* at 168.)

The Commission had to pass upon a substantial number of pieces of conflicting evidence. It had the benefit of the power to examine any witness it wished. It had the assistance of the Secret Service, the F.B.I., the local police and medical and ballistic experts from all over. It was not hurried, but could take months to come to a conclusion. It did not have to act in an atmosphere of courtroom contention. No party to a litigation, civil or criminal, has this opportunity for obtaining objective evidence and no court a chance to give such meticulous consideration as the Commission did.

[284] STOGDILL, INDIVIDUAL BEHAVIOR AND GROUP ACHIEVEMENT 63 (1959).

really mean is that the witness has told a story which meets the tests of plausibility and is therefore credible." [285] This is nothing more than conforming to expectations.

At this point Kalven and Zeisel's finding might be noted to the effect that the prosecution is able to present considerably more witnesses than the defense. The defense witnesses "consist overwhelmingly of the defendant himself, his family and friends, and his character witnesses." [286] This inability of the accused to get more witnesses on his behalf may be due to the unlikelihood of his finding eyewitnesses, whereas the prosecution has the complainant as a witness and others whom the complainant may be able to secure at the scene of the alleged offense. When the accused is a slum-dweller it is usually difficult to induce his friends or neighbors to appear on his behalf because they frequently do not wish to get entangled with the law or to lose time from their jobs by attending a trial.

Between the testimony and the verdict there is still more occasion for refraction of the original incident. At best the reality of the case to judge and jury is a secondhand reality. With respect to the secondhand reality the jurors' individual perceptions, interpretations, and recollections of the individual witness are subject to the same limitations as is the witness's own story. (So too is the judge's when he has to determine the facts where there is no jury or perhaps on a *voir dire.*) Each juror has his own fund of experience that will condition not only his relationship to the witnesses, but his relationship to other jurors as well.

There are several transactions within the jury trial. In addition to the transactions between the initial occurrence and the witness, and those between counsel and the jury, there are those between the witness and the jury, the judge and the jury, and among the jurors themselves. Thus the possibility of alteration in the basic episode — the accident itself or the breach of contract or act of adultery or the theft — pyramids. The problem of perception of the incident by the witness has been dealt with in Chapter I. We can regard the witness-juror problem as similarly governed but subject to the further stress of the adversary proceedings. What applies

---

[285] NIZER, MY LIFE IN COURT 11 (1961); see Liefer, *supra* note 282, at 828.
[286] KALVEN & ZEISEL, *op. cit.* 137.

to a witness's observation and the relation to reality, applies to the juror's observation of the witness's testimony. The unreliability of memory in witnesses is replicated to a large extent in the juryman's memory of the evidence, especially in a case extending more than a single day.

Inasmuch as recall is related to socio-educational status, we can expect that judges would have better recall of the evidence then most jurors; and they would be facilitated in their recall by being permitted to take notes, which jurors are not permitted to do. We could make the hypothesis also that the more highly punitive judges and jurors would have better recall of the evidence than the less punitive judges and jurors. This would not mean that judges, particularly high punitive judges, would tend to reach better conclusions than jurors. Because of their generally higher socio-educational status we could also anticipate that judges would make and rely on more *inferences* as well as better recall of the evidence in making their decisions. Furthermore, it may be that, in spite of the limitations of the jury system already discussed, group decision-making tends to be more successful.[287] These are matters requiring considerable research before accepting the abolition of juries, even in civil suits, to speed and improve the administration of justice, in spite of the serious defects in the jury system discussed in this chapter.

We shall concentrate here on the final stage, that of the jury's deliberations. The numerous psychological factors that are brought into play at these various stages have been explored for comparable situations and are now sufficiently well understood for us to be able to apply them to the particular circumstances of litigation.

The jury's (or judge's) findings of fact are primarily conditioned by the credibility given to one witness or another. But if a juror feels more sympathy for either party, or takes a strong dislike to a witness, that emotional response will affect, if not wholly determine, the weight he gives to the evidence. A juror may not get the necessary support from the disliked or disbelieved witness to resolve a conflict in that witness's favor. If the juror feels that, in any event, the plaintiff is entitled to something simply because

---

[287] Shaw, *Problem Solving by Individuals and Groups,* in READINGS IN SOCIAL PSYCHOLOGY 564, at 574-75 (3d ed. Maccoby, Newcomb & Hartley eds. 1958).

he was injured, he may be unable to discriminate among different degrees of accuracy represented by different stories. The keen and impartial observer, of detached Olympian judgment, is as much of a legal fiction as is the reasonable man.

Dean Green, in discussing such fictions as the "reasonable man" and his "foreseeability and reasonableness," comments:

"... Moreover, if we reflect on these terms we must realize that both the reasonable man and his foreseeability are transparent fictions; their combination in a comprehensive formula is only a technique employed to submit the issue of negligence so that a jury is required to consider the total factual data of a case and determine whether defendant's conduct should be condemned and penalized. They are argumentative words with no definite or literal meaning but are capable of absorbing any meaning given them. This is not to belittle them, for among the numerous fictions that have been employed by the courts until more substantial concepts could be developed the foreseeability of the reasonable man is one of the most valuable. Their value lies in the fact that they accommodate themselves to the particular case with the greatest ease and leave the evaluation of the factual data of the case for the intelligence of the advocate and of the jury." [288]

This sounds reassuring. However, the fiction of foreseeability and the reasonable man can come to haunt us when we consider proof of intent in criminal and tort cases. Foreseeability becomes merged with recklessness, something in which a reasonable man would not engage. The evil of this fiction, this As If, is well put by the English legal scholar Glanville L. Williams. "To begin by requiring intention for a particular crime, and then to say that intention can be inferred from recklessness, is to cheat with words." [289] In other words it is a deceptive fiction of the law to find intention to do a wrongful act from the wrongdoer's recklessness,

---

[288] *Foreseeability in Negligence Law*, 61 COLUM. L. REV. 1401-24 (1961).
[289] THE MENTAL ELEMENT OF CRIME (1965).

that is, behavior without any intention to do something wrongful. In fact the manner in which we derive a conclusion of intention has much that is fictional. Judges were more modest in former days, as in the time of Edward IV, when Judge Brian said "The thought of man shall not be tried, for the devil himself knoweth not the thought of man." [290]

We all tend to think in patterns, and thus if a witness has been a war hero, or is active in church affairs, or is a bank president, we assume not only that he is brave, or pious, or financially reliable, but also that in the entire syndrome which these traits connote, he has other admirable traits including honesty, and further, that he is telling the truth on this particular occasion. We are shocked when a bank official or a religious leader violates social standards because we have come to expect of entire classes of people greater conformity to the goals established for society than of other people. Certain stereotypes serve as our models and heroes, and we measure others by those yardsticks. Our attitudes in general are formed in relation to reference groups which we use as models. [291]

This formation of stereotypes emerges from the search for social constancy as described by Kilpatrick and Cantril. [292] It serves as the basis for our formulation of functional probabilities, just as do the patterns created by our experience on a perceptual level. But these stereotypes are, again, "essentially forms society provides in order to enable a person to get along more effectively with his own being," and are invoked to "bring greater standardizations and predictability to a wide range of behavior as well as to provide some people with common significances." So we must return to the nature of one person's judgment of another as being subjectively conditioned. It is as though each juror had a ruler by which he measured the witnesses, and each ruler was marked in fractions of inches, but they could not be standardized; as if the juries could communicate in terms of inches, but not in fractions, and each fraction means something different to the next juror, and individually and as a group different to any of the others.

---

[290] POLLACK & MAITLAND 474-475 (1911). See also full discussion in MARSHALL, INTENTION IN LAW AND SOCIETY (1968).

[291] See Siegel & Siegel, *supra* note 108.

[292] See Kilpatrick & Cantril, *The Constancies in Social Perception*, in EXPLORATIONS IN TRANSACTIONAL PSYCHOLOGY 354-65, at 357 (Kilpatrick ed. 1961).

When faced with something that he has previously experienced to be "bad," the juror, like the witness, will either not see it, that is, deny its existence, or reorganize his perception so that he can perceive it as bad.[293] The first, of course, is a process of psychological denial already discussed. The other is a tendency toward over-simplification as described similarly by Ross Stagner, who notes that "cues indicative of behavior contrary to our expectations are often distorted to support the rigid percepts already organized. . . . Each tends to see reality only in the manner which is compatible with his own motives and past experiences." [294] This is especially true in cases involving sex which provide the stimuli for the release of hostility which protects the ego from repressed sexual instincts.[295] Cases involving deviants and outgroups afford the opportunity for projection of repressed instincts and hostility in a manner which is safe.[296]

Judges and juries must be presumed to share with other mortals attitudes of aggression toward or withdrawal from deviants and outgroups based on ego defensive needs, particularly where there is "encouragement . . . to its expression by some form of social support." They will also share the prejudices of the socially mobile middle class, when they are of that status [297] — which they usually are.

It is unnecessary to discuss sympathy from the point of view of empirical research or psychoanalysis. Naive psychology deriving out of the experience of each one of us makes clear that we and others are frequently motivated to act and judge out of sympathy. Many of us tend to be for "the underdog," that is, if his behavior is not threatening to our values (middle-class or moral) or to our

---

[293] Bronfenbrenner, *The Mirror Image in Soviet-American Relations, A Social Psychologist's Report*, 17, No. 3 J. SOCIAL ISSUES 45-56 (1961).

[294] Stagner, *Personality Dynamics and Social Conflict*, 17, No. 3 J. SOCIAL ISSUES 28, 33-34 (1961).

[295] Jones, E. & deCharms, *Changes in Social Perception as a Function of the Personal Relevance of Behavior*, in READINGS IN SOCIAL PSYCHOLOGY, *op. cit. supra* note 287, at 102.

[296] The author noticed this phenomenon on a number of occasions when the New York City Board of Education passed judgment in cases of teachers charged with improper sexual conduct.

[297] Katz, *The Functional Approach to the Study of Attitudes*, 24 PUBLIC OPINION Q. 163-80 (1960).

sense of social balance. Nevertheless, another legal fiction is that an emotion such as sympathy must not determine judgment. Judge and jury are expected to be objective, free from the common human trait of sympathy. This doctrine was set forth by the New York Court of Appeals in 1899 in *Laidlaw v. Sage,* where Mr. Justice Martin said:

"... sympathy, although one of the noblest sentiments of our nature ... has no proper place in the administration of the law.... If permitted to make it the basis of transferring the property of one party to another, great injustice would be done, the foundation of the law disturbed, and anarchy result." [298]

It would be a surprising departure to discover a lawyer who did not attempt to get judge and jury to identify with his client out of sympathy.

In the shorthand of over-simplification jurors respond to witnesses in the same manner as witnesses do to the incident itself. Each juror is himself a witness to each witness, perceiving and interpreting the testimony through the lenses he has ground out of his own experience and expectations. Prejudices toward a particular segment of the population to which the witnesses or parties may belong come into play here too, for many stereotypes are pegged to particular economic, racial, ethnic, or religious groups, and most of us are labeled in the eyes of our fellows by at least one of these characteristics.[299]

Kalven and Zeisel found significant differences in sympathy arousal by defendants of various categories. The highest sympathy

---

[298] *Laidlaw v. Sage,* 158 N.Y. 73 (1896). So Russell Sage was not required by judicial process to transfer any of his property to the defendant out of sympathy. It was preserved for him to transfer it to a foundation bearing his name, and to leave in perpetuity the image of one who had sympathy for the poor.

[299] In a sense the law has fostered this outlet for prejudice, for challenges to the credibility of witnesses were still being argued in the 20th Century on such grounds. 3 WIGMORE, EVIDENCE § 937 (3d ed. 1940) cites a line of federal cases in which the circuit courts actually had to rule (all held in the negative) on whether an Indian, a Jew, or most often, a Chinese was per se an incompetent witness. A federal rule required that white witnesses corroborate a Chinese alien's suit for readmittance to the country (*id.* § 2066). It is therefore not surprising that these factors are considered, at least unconsciously, by many judges and jurors.

148   LAW AND PSYCHOLOGY IN CONFLICT

(sympathy index + 17) went to defendants under 21; next to
women defendants (+ 11); next to older defendants (+ 8) and
lowest to black defendants, whose sympathy index was negative
(—7).

According to Kalven and Zeisel, in about two-thirds of all trials,
"The jury could not have been moved in disagreement by any
special response to the idiosyncratic variety of defendants.
Further, there is an interesting symmetry; the defendant is seen
as sympathetic with roughly the same frequency as he is seen to
be unattractive." [300] This may be a nice statistical balance that will
hardly be appreciated by a defendant who is not *sympatico* to a
juror. Nevertheless, the fact remains that we link credibility to
attractiveness or unattractiveness.

Where there is a lack of knowledge or perception of some fact
that we deem necessary to reach a conclusion, this gap will tend
to create in us a sense of incongruity with respect to the remaining
data. Therefore, in order to dispel this incongruity or dissonance,
we try to fill in the gap. Because this gap results from lack of
factual knowledge or perception we try to obtain further data. But
the jury cannot do this once they are in the jury room except
perhaps to have a portion of the testimony read to them. This,
however, may not meet their needs. What happens then is what
happens frequently in other situations. The gap is filled in with
rumor. Frequently this gap in knowledge creates suspicion and
jurymen may create their own rumor or even gossip. This rumor
may act to justify the feeling of hostility the jury has against one
or other of the parties or witnesses or attorneys, or it may be used
to fortify an affirmative feeling toward one of them.[301]

The trial procedure itself can shatter the juror's capacity to recall
what has been said by witnesses, lawyers, and judge. Testimony
is constantly dissected and contradicted and reshaped toward
partisan ends. That is the essence of a trial; it is not a scientific
or philosophical quest for some absolute truth, but a bitter
proceeding in which evidence is cut into small pieces, distorted,
analyzed, challenged by the opposition, and reconstructed
imperfectly in summation. Even the manner in which the evidence
is initially presented affects both the witness and the juror. Careful

---

[300] *Op. cit.* 210-14.
[301] FESTINGER, A THEORY OF COGNITIVE DISSONANCE 286 (1957).

step-by-step direct examination of one's own witness builds up a more complete, but less accurate, story than would an opening question that precipitates a narrative response which will be not only more accurate but more interesting and probably more credible to a jury.

Cross-examination, according to Marston, leads to the least complete picture of what happened,[302] and leading questions were described by Stern as having "well-nigh fatal power." [303] This does not accord with the findings of Marshall, Marquis and Oskamp.[304] The differences probably arise from the application of salience to the facts reported in the latter's experiment.

Then the jury must re-create from all these fragments, interspersed with lawyers' objections, judges' rulings, and other trial procedures, the likeliest version of what happened. This version must be evaluated in the light of instructions from the bench about burdens of proof,[305] reasonable doubt, preponderance of evidence, interpretation of statutes, degrees of crime, fault liability, contributory negligence, and other matters of law.

Judge Frank believed that our entire faith in the jury system was founded on the illusion that the jurors could be expected to understand the law as expounded by the judge and also to understand their role within it: "It is inconceivable that a body of twelve ordinary men, casually gathered together for a few days, could, merely from listening to the instructions of the judge, gain the knowledge necessary to grasp the true import of the judge's words." [306] He quotes Judge Bok's observation that "juries have

---

[302] Marston, *Studies in Testimony,* 15 J. AMERICAN INSTITUTE OF CRIM. L. & CRIMINOLOGY 5, 9-11 (1924).

[303] Stern, *Abstracts of Lectures on the Psychology of Testimony and on the Study of Individuality,* AMERICAN J. PSYCHOLOGY 21, 270-82 (1910).

[304] Marshall, et al. *op. cit.,* note 189.

[305] "Nevertheless, in practice, the specific rules for burden of proof make upon us the impression of vain logical verbalities, — on the whole. They are, inherently, artificial methods of controlling the mind's operations. And when applied by a judge in a form of words which the jury is supposed to put to use in the privacy of its chamber, they are unlikely to have the supposed effect, — or indeed any effect, when they are more than the simplest rules of thumb. Comparing the amount of judicial thought expended upon them, they are probably the least worthwhile part of the rules of Evidence." 1 WIGMORE, EVIDENCE § 8c, at 286 (3d ed. 1940). And see Simon, *op. cit.* 200.

[306] FRANK, J., COURTS ON TRIAL 116 (1949).

the disadvantage . . . of being treated like children while the testimony is going on, but then being doused with a kettleful of law . . . that would make a third-year law student blanch." [307] Judge Geller feels that a jury is deciding the verdict during the course of (especially a long, complicated) trial, and that "a charge at the end of a long trial comes too late. The sensible solution . . . is for [the judge to give] some enlightening instructions on the law as the case goes along, with a final summarizing charge at the end." [308]

In the final stages of most trials, the transactions between the judge and jury work for their mutual protection. The heavy responsibility a juryman must carry in making a judgment ". . . based on his individual insecure intuition, is made easier in the following two ways: First, the judgment rendered is not an individual but a collective one, that of the whole jury; and second, the majorities of penal codes leave it to the learned judge, who, under the protection of the paragraphs of the law, limits their influence on the sentence and thus relieves the jury from a part of their responsibility. One can hardly be surprised to find that the attempt to protect the world of paragraphs by means of the lame intuition of the average layman is not a real way out of the crisis of our judicial system." [309]

Nevertheless, in the Chicago Jury Project, Kalven and Zeisel found that the jury followed the evidence and understood the case. It is possible, however, that in the long anti-trust or tax case this might not be true.[310]

After the evidence, the summations, and charge, the jury retires to uncomfortable quarters to deliberate. This is the phase of litigation about which we know comparatively little. The jury room is a sanctuary into which none may enter, though court factotums have been known to put ear to door. Thus what we know about how juries interact on the evidence among themselves is either deduced from the results of their deliberations, from interviews with them

---

[307] *Id.* at 117.
[308] Geller, *Experiences and Reflections of a Trial Judge,* 21 N.Y. COUNTY A.B. BULL. 118 (1963).
[309] ALEXANDER & STAUB, THE CRIMINAL, THE JUDGE AND THE PUBLIC, A PSYCHOLOGICAL ANALYSIS 41 (rev. ed. 1957). See also Geller, *op. cit. supra* note 308, at 117.
[310] *Op. cit.* ch. II and see Simon, *op. cit.* 175-76.

after judgment or from experimental, simulated situations in which persons "play jury."[311]

We can also make some assumptions based on a general knowledge of group dynamics. Social psychologists are especially aware of the tendency toward uniformity within a group situation. The individual's own opinion is reinforced when he finds others in his group who share it.[312] A snowballing effect makes dissent increasingly difficult as the majority increases. This is especially true of matters that cannot be empirically verified, for as Muzafer Sherif found, when the validity of a hypothesis cannot be tested, its validity is likely to be deduced from the number of people who share in it. Sherif has reported that "in a situation [in which] . . . the individual is unable to tell right [from] . . . wrong, he is almost completely dependent upon the group for selecting a response."[313] The mere existence of dissent rankles, and the desire is for unanimity. Thus members of the majority, continuously addressing themselves to those in the minority, will encourage them to get on the bandwagon and thus increase the security with which the majority view can be maintained. If the determination is unchallenged, there is complete security for all who believe in it. Of course in a legal system which requires unanimity this process will be emphasized.

The forces that function to encourage uniformity include one category defined as helping the group to accomplish its purposes. A jury, to achieve its purposes, must reach a verdict, and a verdict, in most cases, requires unanimity. So here we have two overlapping pressures, one general and one specific, that will hammer out a form of agreement among the jurors.

Cartwright and Zander quote Asch as describing the individual's awareness both of himself and of others in relation to the outside world: "He notes that he, as well as others, is converging upon the same object and responding to its identical properties. Joint action and mutual understanding require the relation of intelligibility and structural simplicity. In these terms the 'pull' toward the group

---

[311] Kalven and Zeisel, Padawer-Singer, and Simon all found their experimental juries to be earnest, conscientious and understanding, behaving unselfconsciously, in every way as genuine juries might be expected to do.

[312] See Festinger, *Informal Social Communication*, in CARTWRIGHT & ZANDER, GROUP DYNAMICS: RESEARCH AND THEORY 286 (2d ed. 1960).

[313] *Introduction* to CARTWRIGHT & ZANDER, *op. cit. supra* note 312, at 165, 167, citing SHERIF, THE PSYCHOLOGY OF SOCIAL NORMS 138 (1936).

becomes understandable," and furthermore, the momentum toward uniformity is within the individual himself, a product of his own uncertainties and need to find harmony with the world around him.[314]

For groups of twelve, it has been reported that the individual has less regard for the value of his own opinion than he does in smaller groups.[315] Saks and Padawer-Singer, however, show that there are other values to twelve person juries that are important.[316] This is presented as a factor that reduces participation as the group increases, especially if the discussion is limited in duration. The pressure to reach a consensus tends to make the individual less determined to maintain his position, thus producing another drive to uniformity. Applying this data, we can be certain that juries do compromise in terms of such matters as guilt, liability, and damages. This desire for harmony is evidenced not only in those cases in which the award is obviously averaged from a number of possible proposals, but also by the ways in which damages will be reduced to compensate for doubts about liability.

The University of Chicago Jury Project suggests that if the fight about liability has been heated, the jury will have exhausted its combative energies and will grasp quickly at some figure for damages. This Project's work also indicates, so far, that juries do consider many of the factors legally forbidden to them in estimating damages, clearly varying the damages awarded with the degree of negligence found, and "where facts as to liability and damages are ambiguous, damages are likely to vary with the number of dependents looking to the plaintiff for support." [317] If this be so, then we can conclude that the law with which the judge charges the jury is another "As If" situation, another legal fiction.

Judges, where they sit without juries, will probably form their

---

[314] *Id.* at 168.

[315] See Hare, *A Study of Interaction and Consensus in Different Sized Groups*, 17 AMERICAN SOCIOLOGICAL REV. 261, 267 (1952).

[316] See note 237.

[317] A complete exposition of this project is by Professor Harry Kalven, Jr., *Report on the Jury Project,* Univ. of Mich. Law School, CONFERENCE ON AIMS AND METHODS OF LEGAL RESEARCH (1955). He begins by noting the ambivalent role of today's jury, as evidenced by the fact that the Federal Tort Claims Act does not provide for trial by jury although the cases may be identical to those tried with a jury except that in the former instance the government is a party. (Compare workmen's compensation cases once uniformly tried by jury.)

judgments in a similar manner. This is an appropriate subject for research before we abolish juries even in civil cases.

The Project's studies also indicate that juries do consider taxability of the award, attorney's fees, interest, and insurance, even though they are not supposed to do so. In one sample case tried before three experimental juries, when the matter of insurance was raised casually at the trial, and was not contested by the defendant's lawyer, the damages awarded were considerably lower than when counsel objected, the objection was sustained, and the judge instructed the jury to disregard what they had just heard. This legalistic byplay had more firmly entrenched in the jurors' minds the question of insurance, so that even though it was raised in a negative context, it was a prominent and formative consideration. The verdict when the insurance matter was raised and ignored was only slightly higher than when it was not raised at all, indicating perhaps that the average defendant in a negligence suit is assumed to be insured, and only when this becomes a major issue does the existence of insurance greatly affect the verdict.

As every lawyer knows, the idea that a party carries insurance need not be crudely presented during the trial. It can be more subtly implanted in the *voir dire* of prospective jurors. So can other biases inadmissible, or perhaps unprovable, at the trial be suggested on the *voir dire*.[318] The case then proceeds to verdict and judgment on the fiction that it is determined on the evidence, As If the biasing on the *voir dire* had never occurred.

Judge Charles Clark, commenting on the Project's report, said that "The jury is too fine, as well as too clumsy and expensive an instrument for all this load (referring especially to the Southern District of New York), . . . it just isn't the correct way to achieve sound policy for the victims of this industrial age and our modern civilization."

There has been much debate as to the value of juries. We need not here enter this controversy. Certainly the area in which the law permits juries to act is severely circumscribed by the judicial charge and the rules of evidence. "Based as they are upon the principles of inductive logic, the philosophy behind them is that

---

[318] See KAPLAN & WALTZ, THE TRIAL OF JACK RUBY 91-92 (1965).

laymen are not logicians and therefore should be prevented from hearing facts from which illogical conclusions are irresistible." [319]

Laymen may not be good logicians. Can they, then, be immune from drawing the illogical conclusions from the evidence of witnesses? Fault liability, the area that contributes the largest number of cases to our congested courts, relies almost entirely on the observations of eyewitnesses or on witnesses who may hear, illusory and unreliable as such testimony may be. Whether their conclusions, based on their premises, are logical or not, their premises are in large measure founded on unreality or derived from the reality of witnesses whose perceptions are in conflict.

It is the principle of fault liability that governs most personal injury litigation. Our traditional method of handling negligence claims is a costly way *not* to accomplish our purpose.[320] The purpose, presumably, is to determine those at fault and compel them to compensate those they have injured; but "... road accidents do not usually have a single 'cause' " and "each individual accident is likely to have several causative factors. ... The search for single causes of accidents is usually likely to prove unproductive." [321] Where, we may ask, is the logic of searching for a nonexistent single cause by taking testimony of misperceptions inaccurately and selectively recalled?

Fault liability is based on fictions. It is these fictions, these As Ifs, that clog our court calendars, not a paucity of judges or calendar practices or pretrial procedures. Consequently *no-fault insurance* makes good sense as a substitute for an outmoded, irrelevant method of determining responsibility, that is, finding fault.[322]

---

[319] STRYKER, *op. cit. supra* note 280, at 35.

[320] Marshall, *The Unreality of Accident Litigation: A Plea for a New Approach,* 50, No. 8 A.B.A.J. 713-18 (1964).

[321] Norman, *Road Traffic Accidents,* 11, No. 12 WORLD HEALTH ORGANIZATION PAPER 19 (1962).

[322] In self-defense we are more concerned with blame than with reality.

"All of a sudden it came to me,
All of a sudden it came:
That half the world is placing
And half avoiding blame."

Dean Wigmore concluded years ago that within the arena of adversary proceedings little will be gained by making better rules.

"Our *judges* and our *practitioners* must *improve in spirit* as a prerequisite for any hope of real gain to be got from better rules. In the end, the man is more important than the rule. Better rules will avail little, if the spirit of using them does not also improve.

"Counsel must become less viciously contentious, more skillful, more intent on substance than on skirmishing for a position." [323]

Wigmore himself apparently believed such a change is unlikely.

". . . to *abolish* the bulk of the rules *now,* in the ordinary courts, would be a *futile* attempt. To pass a law (supposing this possible, in the hasty manner of our legislation) would amount to little or nothing. You cannot by fiat legislate away the brain-coils of one hundred thousand lawyers and judges; nor the traditions embedded in a hundred thousand recorded decisions and statutes. And the plain fact is that trials are today being managed by these men and these books, as the living receptacle of the rules." [324]

What is required is social invention in the law based on findings of the social sciences. As the statements of lawyers already quoted indicate, many of these findings are no surprise to them. But in their operational world they tend to deny the existence of such realities and to focus on the "As Ifs," their legal fictions. This is the lawyer's way of resisting change, of resolving the incongruities between the law and reality.

If, as Dean Wigmore says, it would be futile to attempt to abolish the bulk of our rules — and presumably to adopt new ones that are more realistic — could we not as first steps withdraw from the area of fiction those legal processes which most offend reality and for which acceptable substitutes can be found? Could we not search for ways, wherever practicable, to solve by other methods conflicts now submitted to trial?

---

[323] 1 WIGMORE, *op. cit. supra* note 305, at 263.

[324] *Id.* at 259-60.

CONCLUSION

In a civilization so largely founded on scientific method, and in which daily living is so dependent upon the application of scientific findings, the theory and practice of law remain largely immune to this prevailing cultural pattern. Though science appears in the courtroom at times in the form of evidence, and tests derived from the natural sciences are used in specific cases, those findings of the psychological sciences which apply directly to and challenge the precepts and practices of our courts are largely ignored. It is as though lawyers and judges indulged in the psychological process of denial which has been discussed in connection with witnesses. The law as we practice it is a backwash from the theory of "natural law," which is blocked from contact with the otherwise empirical nature of our culture. "Right" and "wrong" still seem to have a theological connotation of "good" and "bad" more than a scientific one of relativity, situation or predictability.

The conservatism of lawyers is supported by their intellectual and economic vested interest in traditional concepts and behavior which, as with other people, are threatened by change. The common attitude of the bar and political scientists is that knowing these defects in our trial system, the system nevertheless serves a purpose, and is certainly better than the more primitive systems from which it grew. It does not help to make an issue of the assumptions on which our laws of evidence are based. Why disturb the *Als Ob* of the courtroom? Will this not bring the law into contempt?

Of course, our legal procedures as they exist serve social purposes. But it is when they lack validity or reality that the laws will tend to be held in contempt. It should be apparent that our courts are not giving satisfaction today when we see how large a proportion of commercial cases are submitted to arbitration or settled out of court and what a large proportion of negligence cases never reach the courtroom.

Above all, what is indicated is establishment of a closer relationship between law and psychology, and participation by lawyers and psychologists in empirical research into the processes of the law. This is rare, although more frequent today than at any time since the aborted efforts at the early part of this century. It is curious in view of the common deductive approach of both

157

science and law. In the law, however, there is unwillingness to experiment — sometimes for good reasons, dealing as it does with life in the living — but principally, one suspects, because lawyers have intellectual and emotional investment in the fictions of the As If.

Lawyers and scientists have different techniques for fact-finding. This makes it difficult for lawyers to accept and apply the empirical findings of scientists. Of course, scientific testimony by physicians, engineers, chemists, etc. (however suspect it often is), is acceptable within the formalities of our adversary system of litigation.

The history of Anglo-American law and the training of lawyers are embedded in that system. This is distinctly illustrated in *Ballew v. Georgia*.[325] In the court's opinion there was heavy reliance on the findings of social psychologists. In a concurring opinion such reliance was characterized as "reliance on numerology derived from statistical studies." That opinion then went on to say, *"Moreover, neither the validity nor the methodology employed by the studies cited was subjected to the traditional testing mechanisms of the adversary process."* (Italics added.) But the adversary process of the bar is very different from scientific method. In the former, opponents examine and cross-examine those who testify and the goal is to win the case. The adversary system is what the games theorists call a zero-sum game, winner-takes-all.[326] The victory aim of litigation is acknowledged by the American Bar Association:

> "Advocacy is not for the timid, the meek, or the retiring. *Our system of justice is inherently contentious in nature,* albeit bounded by the rules of professional ethics and decorum, and it demands that the lawyer have the urge for vigorous contest." [327] [Emphasis added.]

Scientists, on the other hand, posit certain hypotheses and without taking sides test them. The published results are subject to scrutiny of other scientists and the possibility of replication.

---

[325] 435 U.S. 223, 98 S.Ct. 1029-42 (1978). See also *Williams* and *Colgrove, op. cit.*
[326] RAPOPORT, FIGHTS, GAMES AND DEBATES 262-64 (1961).

[327] The American Bar Association Project on Standards for Criminal Justice — Standards Relating to the Prosecution and the Defense Function, 174 (1970).

They may be challenged and discredited as a result of other research but not by adversaries determined to win. (This does not mean that scientists do not sometimes place themselves in adversary roles and try to win points. This is exceptional and not consistent with the scientific method.) Consequently, the adversary mentality is not appropriate to science. For that matter it may be a barrier to conflict resolution and the achievement of consensus necessary in many areas in which lawyers function.[328]

This is not to denigrate the adversary system in the trial process. It does enable the finders of fact better to determine the credibility of evidence and to clarify issues. Even if all facts are stipulated by the parties the meaning of those facts, their relevance and implications require explication from the several points of view of the parties concerned. This remains an adversary process.

In addition to its advantages as a winnowing process, it has been found in a series of research experiments:

". . . [T]hat a procedure that limits third-party control, thus allocating the preponderance of control to the disputants, constitutes a just procedure. It is perhaps the main finding of the body of our research, therefore, that for litigation the class of procedures commonly called 'adversary' is clearly superior. . . . Moreover, the adversary procedure produces greater satisfaction with the judgment, regardless of the outcome of the case and regardless of the parties' beliefs in their own guilt or innocence." [328a]

The adversary system of the law and the methods of science each has its place in the ecology of human enterprise but they cannot be confused as in the Supreme Court's concurring opinion in *Ballew.*

Moreover, science demands precision but not certainty. Law aims at certainty but lacks precision because its quest for certainty

---

[328] Marshall, *Lawyers, Truth and the Zero-Sum Game,* 47 NOTRE DAME LAW. 919 (1972).

[328a] Thibaut & Walker, PROCEDURAL JUSTICE: A PSYCHOLOGICAL ANALYSIS (1975).

glosses over the innumerable variables of individual and situational diversities, which probably will always cause law to be uncertain. Nevertheless, lawyers tend to dispose of variables and diversities by rationalization and by attempting to fit the individual *man* into a legal formula for *men*.

The man and woman in the street, if he or she would ever think of the science of law, would probably do so in the terms of the poets. Some two centuries ago Charles Macklin wrote: "[T]he law is a sort of hocus-pocus science" and in the nineteenth century Lord Tennyson described it as "The lawless science of our law. . . That wilderness of single instances."

There must still be fought in the realm of law the struggles that philosophy and theology had to go through when confronted by the natural sciences. This is not the first time that science and legal process have been in conflict. Heretics and witches, or better witches and other heretics (for after the 12th Century witches were deemed heretics in most parts of the western world) were tried by methods which today appear horrible and absurd. The *auto-da-fé*, ordeals by fire, hot irons or water as well as oral examinations were the accepted method of inquiry until the 18th Century. Kangaroo courts and lynchings were not uncommon. One of the most ingenious guilt-determining methods of the law was a flotation process in which the opposite thumbs and big toes of the girls were tied together before they were thrown into the water to sink or float. In 1489 the art of the Inquisitors became codified in the *Malleus Maleficarum* or Inquisitor's Manual, "from which they plied their tortured victims with questions and were able to extract such confessions as they desired; by a strange perversion these admissions, wrung from their victims by rack or thumbscrew, were described as voluntary." [329]

In the 16th Century some doubts as to the prevalence of witches and the methods of their prosecution arose. John Wier (or Weyer) wrote two books on the subject which became popular. He was a physician who studied witches, "unmasking the cheaters and the charlatans," and concluded that witches were in fact only mentally deranged old women and not heretics at all. He called for an end to their torture and execution. The more conservative legal minds

---

[329] *Witchcraft*, 28 ENCYCLOPAEDIA BRITANNICA 757 (11th ed. 1911).

of the day who had their intellectual and emotional commitment to the existing methods, that is, the inquisitors and theologians, attacked him and his supporters. Did not the authority of Thomas Aquinas, several popes and ecclesiastical synods support the existence of witchcraft? It was said that thanks to Wier and his followers "the affairs of the Devil were brilliantly progressing." [330]

In the 17th Century, with the establishment of The Royal Society in England, "the whole force of the English intellect was directed to the study of natural phenomena, and to the discovery of natural laws." This resulted in a "general disposition to attribute to every event a natural cause." There followed the conviction that to attribute phenomena to witches was absurd. Nevertheless, in 1664, Sir Matthew Hale, in sentencing two women to be hung as witches, stated that "the reality of witchcraft was unquestionable; 'for first, the Scriptures had affirmed so much; and secondly, the wisdom of all nations had provided laws against such persons, which is an argument of their confidence of such a crime.' " [331]

Here science and law were squarely in opposition. This is a dramatic example of the law declaring "the truth of a proposition" because it is the law. Such logic is, of course, anathema to science but not unknown to law in other instances. Fortunately, science won out, and with the abandonment of the inquisition of witches, witches themselves disappeared. People no longer looked at phenomena with the expectation of finding witchcraft but with the expectation of finding natural causes.

Trial by battle had its day, too — a long day beginning in primitive societies. Well into the 15th Century, before the laws of evidence which we know today were used, a litigant had the right to choose between witnesses — who in fact merely took an oath to the righteousness of the litigant's case — or subjecting himself to an ordeal by combat, either in person or through a substitute. But when the "glorious" days of chivalry passed, the powerful arm or the skilled use of weapons (the contestants perhaps wearing the

---

[330] CASTIGLIONI, ADVENTURES OF THE MIND 253 (1946).

[331] LECKY, HISTORY OF THE RISE AND INFLUENCE OF THE SPIRIT OF RATIONALISM IN EUROPE (1914).

favors of more or less fair ladies) were superseded by judges and juries as a means to determine the truth of the cause. The vestigial remains of trial by battle were trial in a courtroom and dueling. Dueling itself is an example of the confusion by the parties between a search for *justice* and *justification,* which is still an element in litigation.

For how many litigants want *justice* if it does not appear to them to be *justification* evidenced by a judgment, an injunction, or dismissal of the complaint or charge? [332] Certainly this search for justification is a psychological need which ought not to be dismissed lightly or cynically. The question for us, however, is whether it serves society to satisfy such a need in a spirit of contentiousness and the assumption of the law that people hear, see and recall what has occurred without relation to their previous experiences and their expectations. We have noted that this produces testimonial results that contradict or distort reality. Is it to the interest of society, to the interest of a respected judicial system to justify such procedures, as Judge Hale did witchcraft, in reliance upon common practice?

The courtroom has its realities for lawyers, judges, juries, factotums and taxpayers. It also has realities for witnesses and parties — sometimes the grim realities of the punitive aspect of much of the law. But the material with which the court works, the grain or grist to the mill of justice, is a fantasy world of "make-believe" assumptions of As Ifs, as Cardozo referred to them.

It is a Kafkaesque world in which people testify to what they neither saw nor heard accurately, nor recalled nor communicated fully, and in which victory was an end in itself, and men and women compromised to reach a decision which they based upon partially understood testimony, partisan arguments and abstract judicial charges. Life and liberty, property and reputation are staked on bets or guesses as to what really happened.

There is need for joint research by lawyers and social scientists as to the reliability of evidence which depends upon observation and recollection. Such research should also attempt to answer the

---

[332] See ch. VI *supra,* and for special reference to police, see Toch, *Psychological Consequences of the Police Role, supra* note 135.

question: What possible techniques can be used to avoid the distortions now prevalent in testimony? [333] Effort should be made to reconcile the rules of evidence and conduct of trials with what we know about the nature of perception. Courts and lawyers need knowledge and capacity to analyze scientific material so that they will neither ignore it as "numerology" too mystical for consideration at the bar nor accept it as if scientific methodology were a mystique beyond evaluation by the bar.

---

[333] An example of how courts can modify their procedure on the basis of empirical research in which the court participates is the change in the rules relating to pretrial conferences in New Jersey. Questions had been raised as to the effectiveness of the pretrial conferences and the Supreme Court decided to postpone final decision until it had data from a controlled experiment. The results of this experiment are described in ROSENBERG, THE PRETRIAL CONFERENCE AND EFFECTIVE JUSTICE (1964) and were used as the basis for pretrial procedural reform. Delmar, *The Pretrial Conference and Effective Justice — A Review,* 20, No. 5 THE RECORD OF THE ASSOCIATION OF THE BAR OF THE CITY OF NEW YORK 288-93 (May 1965).

APPENDIX

SUGGESTED PROJECTS FOR RESEARCH AND DISCUSSION BY LAWYERS AND SOCIAL SCIENTISTS JOINTLY

1. (a) We know that in all perception and recall there is a selective process which limits the number of items in any field (in any happening) which are perceived and recalled. Does this selective process differ among different socio-educational groups and subcultures of a nation, and if so, how?

(b) Is the selective process different for witnesses, judges and jurors?

(c) Does the selective process differ between participants in a happening and witnesses to it?

2. The adversary nature of the trial procedure puts pressure on witnesses and tends to bias them in favor or against the parties. (a) What is the nature of these pressures and biases and how do they affect recall?

(b) Further research is indicated as to what may be the effects on witnesses of different styles of examination and cross-examination. Similar studies might be made as to the effects on judges and jurors.

(c) Do these effects of direct and cross-examination differ with relation to witnesses who have previously been on the witness stand and those who appear for the first time?

(d) Does the nature of the case make a difference (commercial cases, accident cases, criminal trials, insanity trials)?

3. Witnesses who are not parties to a litigation may be called because they are otherwise involved (as member of family, employee of a party, official of bank or government), or because they have seen or heard the happening which is the subject of the litigation and volunteer to testify, or because they have seen or heard the happening and been subpoenaed. To what extent do they identify with (support consciously or unconsciously) the side for which they are called to testify? Does it make a difference whether

they are witness-participants or otherwise involved in the happening, voluntary or involuntary witnesses?

4. To what extent does prior writing of recall reinforce the accuracy or inaccuracy of recall later testified to orally?

5. We have evidence that police tend to be more punitive than some other groups of the population. There is also evidence that experience in the role of policeman tends to produce characteristic responses to ambiguous situations resulting in the perception of more violence and greater suspiciousness than in other population groups and that the tendency grows stronger the longer one is on the force. To what extent is this greater punitiveness the result of a self-selection process by people seeking police careers, a selective process by those who recruit or choose policemen, or a process of adaptation to the role, the career of policeman, or all three?

6. If high-punitive and low-punitive people recall differently, (a) to what extent will they make more or less reliable witnesses or better jurors?

(b) Is there a difference in the way in which high-punitive and low-punitive witnesses, judges and juries adapt to the adversary conditions of the trial?

7. In order to minimize the effects on recall of the "adversary duel" in the courtroom, (a) how could trial practices be modified?

(b) What changes in trial practices might produce greater objectivity in testimony? (For example, a comparative study might be made of the Anglo-American and continental systems of presentation of evidence and their relative effects on judge and jury.)

(c) What legal procedures could be withdrawn from the courtroom and handled in a different manner in the interest of effective justice (for example, withdrawing motor vehicle accidents from the courts and adopting procedures similar to those in workmen's compensation cases)?

8. What are the effects of judicial charges on the deliberations and determinations of juries, i.e., to what extent are juries influenced by judicial charges in different kinds of cases?

9. (a) Are juries and judges prejudiced by questions put to the jury on the voir dire?

(b) To what extent is the implanting of prejudice on the voir dire minimized when it is conducted by the judge rather than by counsel?

10. In view of the fact that people in authority have influence on the perceptions, attitudes and values of others, to what extent does a police officer, as witness, influence fact-finders as compared with other witnesses? Does he have greater or lesser credibility? Does his color or national origin make a difference?

11. When a lineup is conducted by police officers not connected with the investigation of crime, what effect does this have on the accuracy of identification?

12. What would be the effect on identification by the procedures suggested by Levine and Tapp in footnote 153, page 57, *supra*?

13. Does the stimulating effect of interrogation result in differences in recall over time intervals?

14. What may be the relationship, if any, of the stress of a witness to the accuracy and coverage of his or her testimony?

15. How do witnesses perceive their role and how is this effected by the rituals of the courtroom, such as oaths and expressions of judicial authority?

16. To what extent can a trier of fact be successfully instructed to discount any increase of suggestiveness inherent in the use of leading questions?

17. Will hostility of a partisan witness stimulate better recall or merely encourage him or her to dissemble in order to win a point?

18. What, if any, are the differences in the performances of 8 or 10 member juries as compared with 6 and 12 member juries with respect to verdicts, decision process and population representation?

19. To what extent are judges biased by their previous

experiences, such as having been prosecuting attorneys or attorneys for legal aid societies?

20. What are the effects on witnesses, jurors and counsel of the presence of photographers and television cameras photographing a trial?

INDEX

References are to page numbers.

169